Legal Aspects of Personal Fitness Training

Second Edition

by
BRIAN E. KOEBERLE, J.D.
President, Koeberle & Associates, Inc.
Pittsburgh, Pennsylvania

Second Edition revisions by
DAVID L. HERBERT, J.D.
Partner, Herbert & Benson
Attorneys at Law
Canton, Ohio

With a foreword by
DAVID L. HERBERT, J.D.
Partner, Herbert & Benson
Attorneys at Law
Canton, Ohio

Published by
PRC Publishing, Inc.
4418 Belden Village St., N.W.
Canton, Ohio 44718
(800) 336-0083

ISBN #0-944183-24-7
Library of Congress Catalogue Card #97-075494

Published by:
PRC Publishing, Inc.
4418 Belden Village St., N.W.
Canton, Ohio 44718
(330) 492-6063
(800) 336-0083

TABLE OF CONTENTS

PUBLISHER'S NOTICE

PRC Publishing, Inc.
4418 Belden Village St., N.W.
Canton, Ohio 44718
(800) 336-0083

DEDICATION

This Second Edition, as with the first, is dedicated to my parents, Fred and Rose Marie Koeberle.

Brian E. Koeberle

ACKNOWLEDGEMENT

Special thanks to David L. Herbert for encouraging this work, and providing the Second Edition revisions. Thanks to the staff at PRC Publishing, Inc. for their editorial assistance and preparation of this manual.

Also, to all those in the fitness industry who encouraged and supported me in this endeavor, a heartfelt thanks!

Brian E. Koeberle

FOREWORD

by David L. Herbert, Esq.,
Partner, Herbert & Benson, Attorneys at Law
Canton, Ohio

Since the first edition of this work was published in 1990, the business of personal fitness training has continued to grow at an unprecedented rate. According to some accounts, there are now over 55,000 personal trainers practicing in the United States alone. At the same time, the required degree of training, expertise and concomitant responsibility of such professionals has also grown. More is expected from personal trainers by those seeking and obtaining their services than average health club attendants. To be sure as well, more will be expected of such professionals in the event that a client suffers some untoward incident.

As recognized in the first edition, the rather broad nature of possible services rendered by personal fitness trainers, coupled with the diverse settings within which prescribed and/or supervised activities can be carried out, makes it seem likely that there are certain risks related to the provision of such services beyond those which are inherent in the normal health club setting. A thorough presentation of these risks, together with a practical analysis of professional practices and risk management principles designed to avoid these risks, seems to be desperately needed.

In the seven years that have passed since this work was first presented, the Aerobics and Fitness Association of America (AFAA) the National Strength and Conditioning Association (NSCA) and the American College of Sports Medicine (ACSM) among others, have developed specific training and certification programs for personal fitness trainers. These organizations, along with the American Council on Exercise (ACE), which has maintained such a program since 1990, have trained and certified thousands of professionals since their certifications were developed.

Since the first edition of this work was published, ACSM has also developed and published both its first and second edition of ACSM's STANDARDS AND GUIDELINES FOR HEALTH/FITNESS FACILITIES. Similarly, the International Health, Racquet and Sports Club Association (IHRSA) has also developed its own operational standards and guidelines for member clubs which is now in its second edition. Both of these organizational efforts have gone a long way to "professionalize" the fitness industry and to provide association development of rules and guidelines for professionals to utilize to adhere to the ever changing and developing standard of care. When coupled with the post-1990 certification programs for personal fitness trainers developed by AFAA, ACSM and NSCA the profession of personal fitness training has bloomed and flourished.

Brian E. Koeberle's effort in developing the original version of this work and in assisting with the revisions to this manuscript should go a long way to assist practitioners in this growing and popular profession to recognize their duties, responsibilities and potential risks. Moreover, it should greatly help to alert these individuals to those situations where they need legal, medical or other professional advice. Once alerted to those instances where outside advice is needed, and armed with enough background information to ask the right questions, knowledgeable personal fitness trainers should be in a position to improve the services rendered to their clients while also reducing their own risks of claim and suit.

To develop this important and interesting work, which I have been privileged to update, Brian Koeberle has drawn upon his professional background in both personal fitness training and law. He has been involved in the fitness field since 1983. Starting out as a trainer at a Nautilus Fitness Center in Erie, Pennsylvania, Mr. Koeberle began freelancing as a personal trainer in 1986, starting his own personal training company called "Bodies by Brian." A graduate of the Pennsylvania State University (B.A. 1983), Brian enrolled in law school in the Fall of 1986. While attending law school at Duquesne University in Pittsburgh, Pennsylvania, Mr. Koeberle continued his personal training business. In fact, Brian virtually paid his way through law school as a personal fitness trainer.

While in law school, Brian was Associate Articles Editor of the DUQUESNE LAW REVIEW. He is past president and founder of the Entertainment and Sports Law Society at Duquesne Law School and organized and promoted a highly successful annual Entertainment and Sports Law Symposium while president of that organization.

After graduation from law school in June of 1989, Mr. Koeberle accepted a position as an Associate at the Honolulu law firm of Damon, Key, Bocken, Leong, Kupchak, the same law firm he clerked with during the summer of 1988. Brian hired a personal trainer to operate his Pittsburgh based training company and relocated to Hawaii in June of 1989.

In Hawaii, Mr. Koeberle began practicing law and started Personal Fitness Consultants, Inc., a sports/fitness risk management and consulting firm. Mr. Koeberle is the former Director of Operations of Major League Alumni Marketing, Inc. (MLAM), the marketing and licensing arm of the Major League Baseball Players Alumni Association (MLBPAA). He is currently President of Koeberle & Associates, Inc., a sports marketing and athlete representation firm with offices in Pittsburgh, Pennsylvania. The company specializes in licensing, endorsements, personal appearances, corporate incentive programs, consumer promotions and athlete representation for current and retired athletes.

Mr. Koeberle is also on the faculty of Robert Morris College, teaching a graduate course in Sports Law. He has published articles in *The Exercise Standards and Malpractice Reporter*, and has been appointed to the *Reporter's* Board of Experts as a Consultant on Law and Personal Trainer Liability. Mr. Koeberle has also published various other fitness liability articles in other publications including *IDEA Today.*

Brian also assisted IDEA in its development of the chapter for IDEA's PERSONAL TRAINER MANUAL on the issues of legal liabilities and responsibilities. The MANUAL is used as a study guide for ACE's Personal Trainer Certification program.

During his spare time Brian enjoys weight training, mountain biking, karate, and hiking, as well as music and literature.

As a result of this broad and unique training and background, Brian Koeberle brings a very valuable point of view to typical problems and occurrences in the personal fitness training field. The materials which follow as an updated revision of Brian's work, reflect his knowledge and perspective and should in this new edition, become a valuable updated manual for trainers.

In addition to the legal and professional perspective from which the book has been written, it also presents sound and effective materials for risk management, evaluation of liability insurance needs, the development of a business plan and other useful written materials. This work covers essentially all aspects of professional concern to the personal fitness trainer. It should become an essential reference for anyone interested in pursuing a career in this profession.

David L. Herbert
January, 1998

Chapter 1
INTRODUCTION

The personal fitness trainer has taken the fitness industry by storm over the past ten years. Relatively unheard of outside of the Hollywood set until recent years, the presence of the personal fitness trainer is rapidly becoming commonplace in the fitness world. Estimated at 50,000+ in number, the personal fitness trainer is now found operating in many health clubs and various other facilities and settings across the country. Many trainers are also freelancing on their own, taking fitness out of the traditional gym setting and into the home, office and greater outdoors.

The job requirements and qualifications of the personal fitness trainer are unique to the industry. Drawing upon a wide array of skills and qualifications utilized in all areas of the fitness field, the personal fitness trainer is at times expected to be an expert in a variety of areas. At the same time, however, the trainer needs to be a true generalist. At any one time the personal fitness trainer may be asked to wear many hats – operating as weight trainer, aerobics instructor, fitness "guru," nutritionist, motivator, disciplinarian, counselor, therapist, equipment expert, business person, and overall fitness consultant. Due to this rather unique set of consumer expectations, the personal fitness trainer may be held to a higher standard of care than an average health club attendant. In fact, such a conclusion is undoubtedly likely rather than a mere possibility.

At the same time, the personal fitness trainer needs to be cognizant of the fact that he or she may not "overstep" the bounds of permissible professional practice by entering into the domains of licensed health care providers such as physicians, nurses, psychologists, dieticians, nutritionists or even athletic trainers. This is of particular concern to those trainers who hold themselves out to be experts at providing specific services. With the rapid increase in the number of personal fitness trainers and the related probability that they will be held to a higher standard of care than some others within the industry, comes a probable increase in potential legal liabilities and related exposure to lawsuits due to untoward events and injuries suffered by clients. The number of people entering the field coupled with the fact that there are a number of different standards available for application to personal fitness trainers, leaves the personal fitness training field particularly vulnerable to negligence and related legal claims stemming from the provision of training services. While the development of standards and guidelines by AFAA, ACE, ACSM, IHRSA and NSCA has helped greatly in this regard, there are still many areas of concern.

Leading or encouraging participation in certain fitness activities may in some respects be a high risk business. For example, in 1985, the United States Consumer Products Safety Commission (USCPSC) estimated that there were 43,000 weightlifting related injuries, 19,000 home exercise equipment related injuries, 6,000 informal gymnastics injuries and 30,000 dance related injuries. By 1996 some of these categories rose respectively to 54,000 weightlifting related injuries, 32,000 exercise equipment related injuries and over 34,000 dance related injuries. Moreover, studies conducted in 1984-1985 estimated that 43% of all aerobic dance students and 76% of all instructors had been injured while exercising. *See* Herbert, "Legal Aspects of Fitness Management," *Fitness Management* 22, Nov./Dec., 1987. While more recent USCPSC reports would indicate that this situation is improving, a number of lawsuits have been instituted over the last twenty years against fitness centers and instructors encompassing a variety of claims related to the use of equipment or participation in fitness activities, *see e.g.,* Rabinoff, "An Examination of Four Recent Claims Against Fitness Instructors," *The Exercise Standards and Malpractice Reporter* 2(3):45-47, 1988.

The proliferation and growth of personal fitness training activities while certain claims and litigation related to fitness were making their way through the judicial system pointed out a compelling need for national standards of practice and effective risk management techniques for this subset within the fitness industry, *see* Koeberle, "Personal Fitness Liability: A Trainer's Guide to Legal Fitness," *The Exercise Standards and Malpractice Reporter* 3(5):74-79, 1989. ACSM, AFAA, IHRSA, NSCA and ACE, among others, have sought to fill this need. In 1989, the first ever national conference on one-to-one personal training activities was held. The conference is now an annual event, attracting over 1,000 trainers each year from across the country. AFAA, ACE, NSCA and the NSCA have all now developed and offer certification programs for personal fitness trainers. These organizations have certified thousands of such professionals since 1990.

ACSM in 1990 and again in 1997 published potentially far reaching standards of practice for health and fitness facilities which impact the professional demands placed upon personal fitness training activities as did those which were developed by IHRSA. Of particular import has been the development of certification programs for personal fitness trainers by AFAA and NSCA since 1990. As all of these statements and other national standards begin to emerge to govern this segment of the industry, the professional conduct of the personal fitness trainer will undoubtedly be subject to stricter scrutiny, *see* Herbert, "Who Will Judge Your Professional Conduct In Court?" *The Exercise Standards and Malpractice Reporter* 1(1):14-15, 1987.

In order to effectively minimize the risks of potential legal liability and to keep current with emerging national standards, the successful personal fitness trainer must recognize a need to implement some sort of pre-planning into his or her program. Being an expert in a wide variety of fitness related disciplines will not be enough for the trainer of the future. The successful one-to-one professional will need to have a "hands on" grasp of the complex professional, business and legal questions facing this burgeoning segment of the fitness industry. Such distinct legal questions can run the gamut from the potential legal liability of training clients outdoors to the legal ramifications associated with recommending exercise equipment or to prescribing particular forms or degrees of exercise. Such a "hands on" approach suggests active involvement on the part of the trainer in the risk management process, beginning with the choice of a particular business entity from which to operate and reaching to the formulation of policies and procedures for each area of a typical program. Personal fitness trainers will also need to keep abreast of developments in the industry and stay current as to developing and emerging standard of care issues. Ongoing and continuing education in this regard will be of much import to professionals who desire to stay current and updated in their knowledge base and activities. Those who are certified may in fact be required to pursue such continuing education requirements.

Legal risk management will need to be viewed as a necessary, required phase of the initial and ongoing business planning for any program or service provider. The implementation of such risk management strategies should not be undertaken without consultation with and the active involvement of local program legal counsel and other professionals experienced in legal and other professional aspects of personal training as well as the fitness field in general. The personal fitness trainer who takes an active role in tending to the "legal fitness" of his or her business may well find himself or herself not quite as legally vulnerable as his or her counterpart who posits, "I'll tend to the legal problems when something happens!" In the same vein, however, the personal fitness trainer who stays on top of the legal fitness of the business should be able to provide first class professional fitness training services without letting the fear of lawsuits paralyze professional judgment. The best trainers will be able to balance risk taking with risk management so as to be able to better succeed in the field of personal fitness training. Hopefully, this manual will help personal fitness trainers to achieve that balance, but only when used in conjunction with individualized professional advice.

Chapter 2

BASIC LEGAL CONCEPTS AND TERMINOLOGY

An initial understanding of basic legal concepts and terminology used throughout this manual will hopefully give the reader added insight into those issues dealing with the legal aspects of personal fitness training which shall be examined in the following chapters. Although every effort has been made to present the material in "layman's" terms when dealing with this subject matter, one cannot get around using some basic legal phrases and terminology when explaining specific points of importance. A glossary of common legal terms and phrases has also been provided in the Appendix as an additional reference tool.

THE LEGAL SYSTEM

Many of our present day laws find their origin in the ancient English "common law." The **COMMON LAW** is that body of unwritten laws and principles which derives its authority from custom, usage and judicial opinions. Often referred to as "case law" or "judge-made law," the common law is distinguished from **STATUTORY LAW**, which is the law created by the acts of local, state or federal governmental bodies, such as legislatures. Statutory law is found in constitutions, statutes, codes and ordinances, and is sometimes referred to as "written" or "codified law."

Our legal system is also divided into **CIVIL LAW** and **CRIMINAL LAW**. "Civil law" encompasses a system dealing with private rights, remedies for violations of those rights and the resolution of grievances between individuals. "Criminal law" on the other hand, governs an individual's conduct towards society as a whole, deviations from which are punishable by the government by way of fine and/or imprisonment.

Civil law implications for trainers will usually be governed by the broad law of **CONTRACTS** and **TORTS**, both of which are covered more extensively in this chapter. Potential criminal law implications for trainers can be manifested in **THE UNAUTHORIZED PRACTICE OF MEDICINE** or **THE UNAUTHORIZED PRACTICE OF SOME ALLIED HEALTH PROFESSION**, both of which are also discussed later on in this chapter and in other sections of this work.

Disputes in civil law are typically resolved by the filing of a civil lawsuit. A "civil lawsuit" is instituted by one party (called the "**PLAINTIFF**") against another party (called the "**DEFENDANT**") which seeks monetary damages for alleged wrongs. While the plaintiff is usually compensated monetarily, other relief may also be available in specific instances to command or prevent certain actions. Such actions are often called **INJUNCTIVE RELIEF**.

THE LAW OF CONTRACTS

The law of contracts governs legal rights and obligations among individuals. A **CONTRACT** is an agreement or promise between two or more parties which creates a legal obligation to do or not to do something. A contract is usually a "bargained-for" exchange supported by adequate consideration, *i.e.*, something of value, on both sides. The typical contract involves an "offer" on one side and an "acceptance" on the other. Contracts can be either written or oral, expressed by words or implied by conduct.

In the case of a personal fitness trainer, a contract normally arises when the trainer offers his/her services to a prospective client, promising to perform those services for a fee, which services or promises are accepted by the client who promises to pay or does pay the stated fee. The minute the potential client accepts the offer, a contract is formed. Under the typical arrangement between trainer and client, a **PERSONAL SERVICES CONTRACT** is normally created requiring the trainer to personally perform the services for that client, unless otherwise specified by the parties.

The personal fitness trainer will also need to deal with and understand certain other contracts for other matters he or she will be handling. These other contracts deal with informed consents, liability waivers, assumption of risk documents and other program documents which may all be contracts of one form or another. Moreover, if a trainer desires to hire an associate trainer to perform all or some of the services normally provided by the trainer, the agreement with the associate trainer may also give rise to a contract. If the trainer freelances in a club setting, the agreement between the club owner and the trainer might also be considered a contract. The use of various contracts in the personal training field will be discussed further and in length in Chapters 4 and 5.

THE LAW OF TORTS

A **TORT** is a breach of a legal duty, other than a breach of contract, amounting to a civil wrong or injury for which a court of law will provide compensation in the form of damages. The basic elements of a tort claim are established by proof of the existence of a legal duty to someone, a breach of that duty, and damages or injury occurring as a proximate result of that breach.

A tortious act can be either **INTENTIONAL**, *i.e.,* an act for the purpose of bringing about a particular consequence, or **NEGLIGENT**, *i.e.,* a failure to act or the substandard performance of an act when performance was due. Certain relationships can also give rise to **STRICT LIABILITY**, which deals with the imposition of liability without fault.

Trainers should pay particular attention to the law of torts as it applies to negligent acts. In the event of a tort suit, the trainer's conduct will be judged in a court of law by comparison of the trainer's conduct to the applicable **STANDARD OF CARE**. Under the law of negligence, the standard of care applicable to personal fitness trainers will be that degree of care that a reasonably prudent personal fitness trainer would exercise under like circumstances. This benchmark of behavior is often determined by reference to authoritative standards of practice as established by certain national associations as those standards are interpreted and applied in a court of law during trial by expert witnesses. These standards of practice will be examined in more detail in Chapter3.

Certain statutory duties are classified in law as **NEGLIGENCE PER SE**, a violation of which will create a presumption of negligence. However, in some states, if an injured party contributes at all to his or her injury, he or she may be barred from recovery by reason of his/her **CONTRIBUTORY NEGLIGENCE**. Most states today however, have abandoned contributory negligence systems for negligence cases in favor of a system of **COMPARATIVE NEGLIGENCE**, by which the negligence of a plaintiff and defendant are compared. Typically, pursuant to this system, if the plaintiff's negligence is less than the defendant's, the plaintiff can recover but will have the recovery reduced by the amount of the plaintiff's own negligence. For example, if a plaintiff is 20% negligent and a defendant is 80% negligent, the plaintiff will recover only 80% of what is determined to be the entire damages for the injury.

ASSUMPTION OF RISK is also a total bar to recovery in those states which still follow contributory negligence principles. However, in those states that follow a system of comparative negligence, such a defense is only considered, along with other factors, in determining the related issue of comparative negligence in a given case. A person assumes a risk when he or she voluntarily, and with full knowledge and appreciation of the risks, proceeds with an act despite such risks or dangers. Assumption of risk may be express and valid in some comparative negligence jurisdictions. Express assumption of risk may be incorporated into the trainer's program documents. Assumption of risk forms are explored more fully in Chapter 5, while actual form examples are provided at the end of this work. Assumption of risk may also be implied by law based upon a person's conduct in given circumstances. Even without the actual execution of express assumption of the risk documents, implied assumption of risk concepts may well bar or limit a plaintiff's right to recover in certain cases. It will all depend upon the facts and circumstances of the occurrence and the client's knowledge of the risk which he or she was then undertaking.

The concept of **PREMISES LIABILITY** within the context of tort law should also be of concern to the trainer who comes into professional contact with clients at various sites. The law of premises liability governs the liability of owners and occupiers of land (and buildings) for personal injuries to those who enter upon the land (and buildings). This concept should be of particular concern to both the club trainer and those trainers who instruct clients in the client's home or office, as well as in the outdoors. The law of premises liability is covered in Chapter

7 along with a discussion of liability principles associated with the use and provision of equipment and facilities.

THE LAW OF AGENCY

The law of agency creates a **PRINCIPAL/AGENT, MASTER/SERVANT** relationship. Pursuant to this concept, the agent/servant agrees to act for and be controlled by the principal/master. Under the doctrine of **RESPONDEAT SUPERIOR** the principal/master is liable for the wrongful acts of the agent/servant acting within the scope of his or her authority/employment. The liability created by the doctrine of respondeat superior is one of **VICARIOUS LIABILITY,** *i.e.,* liability without fault. Simply put, pursuant to this doctrine, the principal or employer will be liable for the authorized acts or omissions of the agent or the employee. If the agent or employee is deemed to be liable so will the principal/employer, so long as the agent or employee was acting on behalf of the principal/employer and within the scope of his or her authority.

The personal fitness trainer who accepts employment as an employee of a club or other entity would be subject to the master/servant, principal/agent relationship described above. While the concept of respondeat superior attaches liability to the employer (master/principal) for the torts of the personal fitness trainer (servant/agent), this is only so if the personal fitness trainer is acting within the "scope" of his or her employment. The trainer who acts outside the scope of his or her employment would incur **sole** liability for his/her wrongful acts. While "scope of employment" is sometimes broadly construed, acts outside the scope of the trainer's employment might include teaching a contraindicated exercise, freelancing outside of a club environment as a private trainer or engaging in impermissible sexual activity with a client.

Not all club/trainer relationships give rise to a master/servant, principal/agent relationship. Many clubs hire **INDEPENDENT CONTRACTORS** to provide personal training activities. An independent contractor contracts to do something for another, but is not controlled by the former nor subject to the other's control with respect to the physical performance of the work. In other words, the club owner may contract for an end result, but does not control the means by which the trainer accomplishes that result.

An independent contractor may or may not be an agent. Where an independent contractor is not an agent, the club owner generally will not be directly liable for the torts of the independent contractor/trainer. But, liability may attach to the club owner for the negligent hiring of the independent contractor/trainer, where there has not been an adequate investigation of the trainer or where unqualified people have been hired to provide services. Under other circumstances, a club owner may also be liable under concepts of **"ESTOPPEL"**, pursuant to which the law simply declares that a club owner may not claim that another is an independent contractor or under principles of "**OSTENSIBLE AGENCY**" where a personal fitness trainer may reasonably appear to third parties to be an agent of another. Generally, under these doctrines, the law imposes liability where there are societal considerations for doing so – *e.g.,* there is a reason for a client to believe that the agent was employed by and rendering service for the principal and that the client therefore relied upon the principal's reputation and name, who should not, after injury, be allowed to claim that the agent was an independent contractor for whom the principal had no responsibility. In a circumstance where patrons believe they are receiving service from the club, the club may be estopped from denying that service was actually rendered by a third party.

The test for determining independent contractor versus employee status is discussed further in Chapter 4.

THE UNAUTHORIZED PRACTICE OF MEDICINE

While the foregoing discussion has dealt with the concept of **civil** liability, the personal fitness trainer should also be aware of some of the potential criminal implications involved in personal fitness training, most notably **THE UNAUTHORIZED PRACTICE OF MEDICINE** and/or **THE UNAUTHORIZED PRACTICE OF SOME ALLIED HEALTH PROFESSION**. States have statutorily defined the practice of medicine and certain allied health professions and have provided for the licensing of such professionals. While such statutes prohibit the unauthorized practice of medicine by negative implication, some states have gone as far as statutorily defining and prohibiting unauthorized practices under the penal sanctions of criminal law. Many of these statutes outline the criminal penalties for engaging in the prohibited practices.

Generally speaking, in addition to the potential criminal liability created by reason of a trainer's violation of such statutes, civil liability for unauthorized practices could somewhat "automatically" attach in the event of harm, if any of the personal fitness trainer's services overlap or infringe upon any of the statutorily defined professions which require licensing by the particular state where services are rendered. Although this concept is discussed in detail in Chapter 6, it is important to note early on the potential implications that could be involved in exercise testing and prescription, nutritional counseling, and related services offered by the personal fitness trainer. *See* Herbert, "Are Nutritionists Engaged In The Unauthorized Practice Of Medicine?," *The Exercise Standards and Malpractice Reporter* 2(5):85-91, 1989. Such concepts could also attach to some personal fitness trainers practicing in some states where the use of the term trainer, even perhaps when prefaced by the qualifying words "personal fitness", is prohibited except by those who are licensed as "athletic trainers" or "trainers" providing defined athletic services to athletes.

Where an individual is found to have engaged in such an unauthorized practice and harm results to another within his or her care, the personal trainer may be held to a higher standard of care than that of his or her profession, *i.e.,* that of a licensed professional acting under the same circumstances. Such a comparison will almost always result in a finding of negligence against the professional. In those states where a violation of a statute is deemed to be negligence *per se,* a finding of negligence under these circumstances may be nearly automatic. Personal fitness trainers in these instances may also be enjoined from engaging in such unauthorized activities and may be prohibited from using the term "trainer" unless they are licensed as such.

FINAL THOUGHT

The foregoing legal concepts and terminology should set the groundwork for an examination of the materials which follow. While every effort has been made to present the material which follows within an easily understood lay format, reference to the glossary at the end of this work or to this chapter can be made at any time for further clarification of the legal terms and concepts used throughout this manual.

Chapter 3

STANDARDS OF CARE AND COMPETENCIES FOR PERSONAL FITNESS TRAINERS

A majority of the fitness industry has traditionally resisted attempts at federal and/or state legislation aimed at licensing fitness professionals. Opting instead for "self-regulation" within the field, the industry has favored national certification standards developed by leading national fitness organizations. While this position may change with many opting for licensure in the years to come, *see e.g.,* Sol, "Certification or Licensure of Fitness Professionals: The Debate Begins," *The Exercise Standards and Malpractice Reporter* 4(5):65, 67-68 (1990); "Louisiana Licenses Clinical Exercise Physiologists," *The Exercise Standards and Malpractice Reporter* 9(4):56-59, July 1995, it is certainly clear that national standards of practice and certification programs dramatically impact the fitness industry.

National standards have been promulgated by industry leaders including the American College of Sports Medicine (ACSM), IDEA, the International Association of Fitness Professionals, the Aerobics and Fitness Association of America (AFAA), the National Strength and Conditioning Association (NSCA) and the American Council on Exercise (ACE). The ACSM has a wide range of relevant certification examinations encompassing the

Health/Fitness Director®, Health/Fitness Instructor™ and Exercise Leader™. In 1996, ACSM also developed an Advanced Personal Trainer Certificate of Enhanced Qualifications. AFAA now offers certifications for exercise professionals in step aerobics, resistance training, group exercise, fitness practitioner and personal fitness training. This organization, founded in 1983, has to date certified over 125,000 fitness professionals. AFAA, which is a member of the National Organization for Competency Assurance (NOCA), requires both a written and practical examination for certification. AFAA has extensive resources available for study programs for certification examinees, including a new manual due out in late 1997 or early 1998 tentatively entitled **THE FITNESS PRACTITIONER**. AFAA also has a number of other resource materials available, including its 1995 publications, **AFAA FIRST AID FOR THE FITNESS PROFESSIONAL** and **FITNESS THEORY AND PRACTICE**, and its 1994 work **AFP CODE OF ETHICS**.

AFAA's stated goal is *"to provide quality fitness professionals who are committed to the enhancement of the physical, mental, and overall optimal wellness of every client, to provide continuing education programs, to continue to address standards of competency and practice parameters for fitness professionals, and to provide exceptional customer service, innovative fitness products, and safe progressive fitness programs worldwide."*

AFAA has developed a Code of Ethics for its Fitness Practitioners$_{TM}$ which provides as follows:

"I do hereby attest to maintain the ethical and practical role of an AFAA Fitness Practitioner™.

- *I will uphold all of the Standards and Guidelines established by the Aerobics and Fitness Association of America.*
- *I acknowledge the boundaries of my expertise as a fitness educator and exercise consultant.*
- *I will withhold personal judgment and be an unbiased advocate for lifestyle change.*
- *I will maintain responsibility and accountability to my clients while respecting their confidentiality.*
- *I accept the challenge of my professional growth and will update my practical and theoretical foundations through continuing education.*
- *My overall goal as an AFP is to facilitate "Fitness Management for life™."*

ACE, like ACSM and AFAA, also offers a Personal Trainer Certification provided through examination. Since 1990 ACE has certified more than 23,000 personal trainers. It has developed and published its 1996 PERSONAL TRAINER MANUAL and has published its own code of ethics. Its code in this regard provides as follows:

"ACE-certified Professionals will endeavor to:

- *Provide safe and effective instruction.*
- *Provide equal and fair treatment to all clients.*
- *Maintain an understanding of the latest health and physical activity research and its applications.*
- *Maintain current CPR certification and knowledge of first-aid services.*

- *Comply with all applicable business, employment and copyright laws."*
- *Uphold and enhance public appreciation and trust for the health and fitness industry.*
- *Maintain the confidentiality of all client information.*
- *Refer clients to more qualified fitness, medical or health professionals when appropriate.*

IDEA, which has a personal trainer membership of more than 8,000 (out of an estimated 55,000 U.S. based personal trainers) also has a code of ethics. The code provides standards of expected behavior which provide as follows:

> *"As a member of IDEA, the membership organization of the health and fitness industry, I will be guided by the best interests of the client and practice within the scope of my education and knowledge. I will maintain the education and experience necessary to appropriately train clients; will behave in a positive and constructive manner; and will use truth, fairness and integrity to guide all my professional decisions and relationships.*

1. ***Always be guided by the best interests of the client.***

   a. A personal trainer's primary responsibility is to the client's safety, health and welfare; this responsibility should never be compromised by the trainer's self-interest, personal advantage or monetary gain.

   b. Products or services should be recommended only if they will benefit the client's health and well-being, not because they'll benefit the trainer financially or occupationally.

c. If recommending products or services will result in the trainer's financial gain, disclosure to the client may be appropriate.

d. The number of training sessions should be based on the client's needs, not the trainer's financial statement.

2. ***Maintain appropriate professional boundaries.***

a. A personal trainer should not sexually, economically or otherwise exploit his or her professional relationship with a supervisor, employee, colleague or client.

b. A trainer should respect a client's right to privacy. A client's conversations, behavior, results and – if appropriate – identity should be kept confidential.

c. Physical touching should be used appropriately during training sessions, as a means of correcting alignment and/or focusing a client's concentration on the targeted area. The use of touch should be immediately discontinued at a client's request or if the client displays signs of discomfort.

d. A personal trainer should focus on the business relationship, not a client's personal life, except as appropriate.

e. When a trainer is unable to maintain appropriate professional boundaries or to work within the legitimate agenda of the training relationship – whether because of the trainer's attitudes and behaviors or those of the client – the trainer should either terminate the relationship or refer the client to an appropriate professional, such as another trainer, a medical doctor or a mental health specialist.

f. Sexually oriented banter and inappropriate physical contact should be avoided.

3. ***Maintain the education and experience necessary to properly train clients.***

   a. A personal trainer should continuously strive to keep abreast of the new developments, concepts and practices essential to providing the highest-quality services to clients.

   b. A trainer should recognize his or her limitations in services and techniques, and engage only in professional activities that fall within the boundaries of her or his professional credentials and competencies. Clients should be referred to other professionals for issues that fall beyond the boundaries of the trainer's profession or current competencies.

   c. Health screening, assessment, prudent progression and exercise technique should follow the standards outlined by professionals in the fields of medicine and health and fitness.

4. ***Use truth, fairness and integrity to guide all professional decisions and relationships.***

   a. In all professional and business relationships, a trainer's behavior should clearly demonstrate and support honesty, integrity and trustworthiness.

   b. A trainer should accurately represent her or his qualifications.

   c. Advertising materials should be truthful and fair. When describing personal training services, a trainer should be guided by the primary obligation of helping clients develop informed judgments, opinions and choices. Ambiguity, sensationalism, exaggeration and superficiality should be avoided.

d. Contract language should be clear and understandable.

e. Pricing and procedural policies should be administered consistently.

f. A trainer should never solicit business from another trainer's client. Interactions with clients of other trainers should be open and honest, so that those clients could not interpret the interactions as solicitation of their business.

g. A trainer who works for a business that finds and assigns clients to the trainer should recognize that the clients belong to that business.

5. ***Show respect for clients and fellow professionals.***

a. A personal trainer should act with integrity in his or her relationships with colleagues, facility owners and other health professionals to facilitate the contribution of all professionals to the achievement of optimum benefits for the client.

b. A trainer should never discriminate based on race, creed, color, gender, age, physical handicap or nationality.

c. When disagreements or conflicts occur, the trainer should focus on behavior, factual evidence and nonderogatory forms of communication, not on judgmental statements, hearsay, the placing of blame or other destructive responses.

d. Fitness information should be presented completely and accurately to help clients make informed decisions.

6. ***Uphold a professional image through conduct and appearance.***
   a. Smoking, substance abuse and unhealthy eating habits should be avoided.
   b. Speech and attire should be appropriate to the client's comfort."

The NSCA also certifies Personal Trainers through their successful completion of an examination and practicum. NSCA is accredited by the National Commission for Certifying Agencies of Washington, D.C. To date NSCA has certified over 1,000 personal trainers. Examinees for its certification examination may prepare for NCSA's test through listening to audio tapes, reading its 1995 publication **ESSENTIALS OF PERSONAL TRAINING** and its 1994 publication **ESSENTIALS OF STRENGTH TRAINING AND CONDITIONING**.

Other organizations including the Cooper Institute of Aerobics Research (CIAR), the National Federation of Professional Trainers and the National Association for Fitness Certification also engage in training, education and/or certification of personal fitness trainers.

To one degree or another, all of these educational or certifying groups provide information to those desiring to provide services as personal fitness trainers or to be certified as such. Educational areas offered by these groups involve screening, exercise program development and leadership, ethical and legal considerations, emergency response planning and execution and a number of other areas.

For the personal fitness trainer, certification may become another criteria through which their professional conduct will be judged. If that is the case, both trainers and employers will want a measure of confidence that one of the certifications is legally defensible in a court of law and that it will withstand the scrutiny of expert testimony. *See* Marks, "Is Your Fitness Instructor's Certification Legally Defensible?," *The Exercise Standards and Malpractice Reporter* 2(4):53, 1988; Herbert, "Who Will Judge Your Professional Conduct In Court?," *The Exercise Standards and Malpractice Reporter* 1(1):14, 1987. National certifications from authoritative organizations providing service and education on a respected, national level may very well provide that minimum level of presumptive competency arising out of such a certification in the event of lawsuit.

DEGREES, CONTINUING EDUCATION, AND EXPERIENCE

While certification lends an air of presumptive competence to a trainer's credentials, the trainer should not be content with just certification. If the trainer has a degree in an exercise related discipline, along with continuing education and experience in the field, such qualifications might also be used to judge the competence of a trainer under any given circumstance.

The trend in the field appears to be moving towards either having a degree in an exercise related discipline, and/or certification by an established certifying body. In either event, education appears to be the key toward demonstrable competence, whether one has a formal degree or the appropriate certification. Yet, education acquired through attaining either a degree or certification program may not be enough. A program that requires continuing education credits (CECs) may be necessary to maintain a minimum level of competency. The acquisition of CEC's helps to ensure that the trainer is staying current in this ever changing field.

Most certifying organizations require a certain number of CECs to maintain current certification and good standing. To achieve this result, specified activities are encouraged, including attendance at a multitude of national, regional and local seminars and lectures for the trainer to satisfy the continuing education requirements.

Along with educational background and certification, experience for the personal fitness trainer is a must. All available education may not necessarily guarantee that one will be a competent personal trainer. This is particularly true of the personal training field which relies so heavily on the relationship and bond formed between client and trainer. A good technician will not necessarily be a good trainer. Experience in the field is important to develop the "intangibles" of personal training which have been discussed herein.

Some academic programs have internships that place their students in wellness centers, sports medicine departments, and health clubs. It would be advisable to work one-on-one with clients in this type of formalized setting before branching out to individual practices. Another argument for prior experience is in the fact that most credible certifying bodies require either a minimum of a bachelors degree in a related exercise science discipline and/or a certain minimum period of practical experience.

WHAT IS THE STANDARD OF CARE?

Presently, there are no state or national laws that mandate either licensing, certification or a minimum educational level in order for a personal fitness trainer to apply his or her trade. While there are licensing laws for exercise physiologists in Louisiana, that is the only state (to date) to license any segment of the fitness industry (although bills have been proposed in the state of California to do so). In short, any individual, qualified or not, can legally purport to be a personal trainer or a "fitness expert". However, the state of Mississippi has recently taken the formal position that only state licensed athletic trainers may use the term "personal trainer" or "trainer" in that state.

At present there is no one national organization that sets the standard of care for personal trainers. Rather, the industry has had to rely on a wide array of opinions from a diverse group of organizations. Although these various standards at times overlap one another, they also come into conflict on many occasions. Organizations such as IDEA, ACE, AFAA and the National Council of YMCAs may take a more "fitness" oriented position concerning standards, while groups such as the ACSM (which also addresses fitness) and even the American Heart Association (AHA) may be geared more towards the cardiac rehabilitation and exercise testing end of the scale. With groups such as the American Medical Association (AMA) and the American College of Cardiology (ACC) also promulgating standards, the industry's standard of practice could arguably take on a medical look, especially with certain client populations.

See Herbert, "Keeping Up With The Changing Standard of Care," *The Exercise Standards and Malpractice Reporter* 3(3):37, 40 1989; "An Overview Of The Standards Of Practice For Preventive, Rehabilitative And Recreational Exercise Programs," *The Exercise Standards and Malpractice Reporter: Lawyer's Edition* 1(1):7-9, 1987; THE STANDARDS BOOK FOR EXERCISE PROGRAMS (PRC Publishing, Canton, OH 1992 Supplemented 1993.

Should a personal fitness trainer's professional conduct ever be questioned in a court of law, expert testimony more than likely will be used to determine what is the given standard of care in a particular setting, whether that standard of care has been adequately met, and whether specific conduct fell below that standard. *See* Herbert, "Who Will Judge Your Professional Conduct In Court?," *The Exercise Standards and Malpractice Reporter* 1(1):14, 1987. The divergence of opinion on the standard of care for fitness professionals and personal trainers in particular makes this a difficult process, both for the trainer trying to maintain that standard, and for a court of law trying to interpret and determine the appropriate standard of practice to be applied in given circumstances.

While it appears that a number of organizations are attempting to set the national standard for personal trainers, it still remains to be seen whether or not any one organization may promulgate a standard which will become the national standard to apply in the event of a claim or suit. Whether certification will be accepted as part of the national standard by both the industry and the courts will be the subject of debate by fitness organizations, professionals and experts qualified to testify on the subject during litigation. Such determinations may come in the future.

For the time being, trainers may find themselves in a precarious position. With no clear-cut national standard at this time, trainers may need to ensure that their professional conduct holds up under the most vigorous scrutiny. This is not an easy task when one considers the potential conflicts involved in defining a trainer's professional conduct within the context of existing standards of practice.

Perhaps the most prudent course for the trainer to take at this time is to attempt to follow the historical patterns involved in most professional standards of care. Be it lawyers, accountants, doctors, or other health care professionals, all have had to demonstrate a minimum level of competency through a process of formal education, state licensing, and a system of continuing education. For the trainer concerned about meeting the present ambiguous standard of care for fitness professionals, that pattern could include formal education in the form of a degree in an exercise science related discipline, certification by a national certifying body such as AFAA, ACE, ACSM or the NSCA, and continuing education through various national fitness organizations. Keeping up with current expectations of care as expressed through various association statements as well as current litigation filings and court decisions should also do much to assist the trainer in attempting to keep up with the duty of care owed to the client.

What should be somewhat clear is that personal fitness trainers will probably be held to a higher standard of care than other fitness professionals delivering leadership or instructional services in, for example, health club settings. At least one recent case from the state of Washington, Shields v. Stay Fit, Inc., 903 P.2d 525 (Wa.App. Div. 3 1995) seems to indicate that such a legal scenario could be possible. Given the extra training, education and certification that many trainers have to undergo and the "extra" or higher fees often paid to facilities or professionals for the provision of personal fitness training services, such a conclusion is likely.

FINAL THOUGHT

For the trainer, standards may be used to judge his or her competence in a court of law. For the employer, certification, degree status and experience should be the criteria used for hiring decisions. For the consumer, the trainer's qualifications should be used as guidelines when shopping for the services of a personal trainer. For the court system, standards will be used to compare trainer conduct with the expressed standard of care in specific cases. In any event, the trainer, the employer and the consumer, as well as the industry as a whole, should recognize that the foregoing standards and qualifications are the only available methods of determining a minimum level of competency for a particular trainer. The judicial system in the event of claim and suit will be the final interpreter of what standards apply and under what given circumstances.

Chapter 4

BUSINESS STRUCTURE

The basic business structure within which a personal fitness trainer operates can both affect and afford protection to the business and the trainer. Depending upon the business structure adopted and the business and risk management strategies implemented for that structure, the risk of liability and the potential for loss can be minimized. The development of a comprehensive business plan should be the trainer's starting point. The planning of the business structure should be developed with the advice of legal counsel and a CPA, and should include decisions as to the operational form for the business, the adoption of a business plan, the various business forms to be adopted and contracts to be utilized, a determination to use either (or both) independent contractors or employees, and a selection of the insurance needs for the business. A discussion of each of these concepts follows.

BUSINESS PLAN

Every trainer who decides to develop a personal training business should develop a business plan to use as a road map for managing the business in a prudent and legally effective manner. A business plan has two basic functions; first of all, it can provide the trainer with a blue-print for short-term and long-term planning and strategy. Secondly, it can be presented to investors and bankers in order to secure financing. A business plan like the business itself is a dynamic tool, and should be constantly updated to reflect change and growth within the business.

A business plan should also contain step-by-step plans and strategies for protecting both the professional and the business from liability. A business plan is an excellent vehicle to use to formulate and implement risk management strategies and policies. The trainer inexperienced in writing a business plan can seek guidance at most community, college or university small business development centers. Many of these centers are funded by the Small Business Administration (SBA) and will provide consultation to a small business, as well as assistance in preparing a business plan, often free of charge or for a nominal fee.

The materials which appear on the next two pages are offered as a basic business plan outline that can be used to guide a trainer in this planning process. It is important however to emphasize that this should not be a one time undertaking. Business planning is an ongoing process, subject to such modification and revision as is necessary to meet ongoing market and industry dynamics. The actual plan itself should probably be reviewed at least quarterly if not more frequently. Relevant modifications to the plan, especially to those areas which may expose the personal fitness trainer to new areas of potential liability or the development of new and legally significant forms or documents should be reviewed by legal counsel prior to use or implementation. Those areas which are potentially tax related should also be reviewed by the trainer's accountant, while those areas which may affect risk should be reviewed by a lawyer, risk manager and/or an insurance agent.

SAMPLE BUSINESS PLAN OUTLINE

I. SUMMARY
- a. Mission Statement
- b. Goals and Objectives
- c. Key Personnel Profile
- d. Capitalization Needs
- e. Financial Projections

II. THE BUSINESS FORM
- a. Characterization
- b. Legal Form
- c. Taxable Form
- d. Goals and Objectives

III. PRODUCTS/SERVICES
- a. Description
- b. Potential For Growth/Development
- c. Proprietary Rights
- d. Unique Technologies/Skills

IV. MARKET ANALYSIS
- a. Market Identification and Analysis
- b. Industry Profile and Trends
- c. Market Profile
- d. Competition Profile
- e. Evaluation of the Market

V. STRATEGIC MARKETING PLAN
- a. Target Markets
- b. Projected Sales/Market Share
- c. Service Policies/Product Warranties
- d. Pricing Policies
- e. Sales Strategy
- f. Sales Management Organization
- g. Distribution Plans

VI. OPERATIONS PLAN
a. Location: region, city, site
b. Facility Layout/Improvements
c. Operations Strategy
d. Labor Needs

VII. MANAGEMENT PERSONNEL
a. Organizational Chart
b. Ownership/Methods of Compensation
c. Key Personnel - Contractual Relationships
d. Board of Directors/Advisors
e. Support Services
f. Employee Training Programs

VIII. FINANCIAL DATA
a. Past Income Statements, Profit and Loss Statements, Cash Flow Statements, and Balance Sheets (2-3 years)
b. Projected Income Statements, Profit and Loss Statements, Cash Flow Statements, and Balance Sheets (2-3 years)
c. Projected Break Even Point
d. Capitalization Needs
e. Proposed Capital Structure and Debt/Equity Ratio

IX. EXHIBITS
a. Contract Forms For Clients - Service
b. Contract Forms For Clients - Equipment
c. Contract Forms For Employees/Independent Contractors
d. Informed Consent Forms, Releases/Waivers, Assumption of Risk Forms
e. Client Activity Plans/Prescriptions and Progress Notes
f. Equipment Inspection/Maintenance Records

BUSINESS ENTITY

The personal fitness trainer who freelances will need to consider how the business will operate and under what form. There are three relevant choices: corporate, partnership or sole proprietorship. There are various pros and cons involved in each of these business structures. The costs and expenses associated with the foundation and operation of each vary greatly, with the sole proprietorship being the least costly and the corporation being the most expensive.

A **SOLE PROPRIETORSHIP** is the least expensive of the three business entities to organize and operate. Normally, all that is required of one organizing a sole proprietorship is the registration of a trade name if the business is to be operated under an assumed or fictitious business name, and in some jurisdictions a vendor's license or permit. A sole proprietorship is not considered a legal entity apart from its owner and therefore any profits of the business are taxed directly to the individual owner.

While this structure is the easiest and least complex to organize and operate, it also leaves its owner open to claims of personal liability arising out of business operations - for both contracts and negligence. Since the sole proprietorship is not considered a separate and distinct legal entity apart from its owner, that owner remains personally liable for all business debts and liabilities, as well as for untoward occurrences for which the trainer is deemed responsible.

A **PARTNERSHIP** quite simply is "an association of two or more persons to carry on, as co-owners, a business for profit," Uniform Partnership Act. Partners share equally in the profits of the business unless the parties expressly stipulate and agree upon a different share of the profits. Unless otherwise agreed, partners also share equally in the management rights and obligations of the partnership, and are each jointly and severally liable for partnership debts and liabilities, and for the acts of the other partner(s) which may lead to injury and liability.

In the case of a **LIMITED PARTNERSHIP**, limited partners generally contribute capital to a general partner for the general partner's management of the business. The limited partners are not personally liable for partnership debts and liabilities, and are only at risk to the extent of their respective capital contributions. While the limited partner escapes personal liability, the limited partner cannot take part in the management of the business affairs. Usually, a limited partner contributes money and/or assets as a "silent" partner while the general partner operates and manages the business.

Partnerships are creatures of state statutes. All states have adopted in some shape or form the Uniform Partnership Act (UPA) and the Uniform Limited Partnership Act (ULPA) to govern the relationship of partners. Like the sole proprietor, partners are taxed individually in such proportions as they have previously agreed as to the profits of the firm. Since partnerships are governed by state statutes, a greater degree of formality is required to organize the basic business structure than is required of the sole proprietorship.

A **CORPORATION** on the other hand is a legal entity separate and apart from its shareholders/owners. Since a corporation is a separate legal entity, it can sue and be sued, enter into contracts, own property and so forth just the same as an individual. One of the main advantages of the corporate form is that it offers its shareholders/owners limited personal liability for the corporation's debts and liabilities. The shareholders are only at risk to the extent of their capital contributions as to these obligations, unless they personally guarantee such debts. Thus, the trainer with personal assets can be protected under the corporate form from personal losses in the event of corporate liability.

The main drawback of the corporate form of business is the complexity in establishing and operating the business as well as being subject to double taxation, as we shall discuss hereafter. Corporations like partnerships are created and governed by state statutes. The corporation must operate in accordance with its charter and bylaws. The corporation must also elect and appoint directors and officers to oversee and run the business. A court of law might "pierce the corporate veil" and impose liability upon shareholders directly if a corporation is not operating within the law and pursuant to the formalities that govern corporations. If that is the case, the corporate form will be disregarded and the shareholders/owners would become personally liable.

Corporations, unlike partnerships and sole proprietorships, are subject to double taxation. Profits are taxed once at the corporate level, then again when any money is distributed to the shareholders in the form of dividends or salaries. An alternative solution to this problem of double taxation would be to form an **"S" CORPORATION**. An "S" corporation is taxed like a partnership or sole proprietorship inasmuch as all profits or salaries are taxed directly to the shareholders with the corporation filing information returns only. Despite this comparison, this form of business entity still retains the other benefits of the corporate form such as limited liability. There are certain restrictions on the formation of an "S" corporation and certain formalities as to its organization which should be discussed with both legal counsel and a CPA prior to opting for such a business structure. For a comparison of the various business entities as well as their respective advantages/disadvantages, the following charts should be reviewed.

BUSINESS ENTITY COMPARISON CHART

	Sole Proprietor	Partnership	Corporation	S-Corp.
Ownership:	individual	two or more partners	unlimited number of shareholders	number of shareholders limited to 35
Formalities:	none, except tradename registration	usually filing of certificate of limited/ general partnership	usually filing of articles of incorporation with state office	same as corporation
Liability:	unlimited personal liability	unlimited joint and several personal liability; limited liability for limited partners	limited liability	same as corporation
Existence:	terminates upon death/ disability of owner	usually specified term or by death/legal disability/ withdrawal/ insolvency of general partner	usually perpetuity	same as corporation
Management:	by owner	by general partners	by board of directors	same as corporation
Taxation:	owner taxed on profits	partners taxed on share of profits	corporation taxed on profits; shareholders taxed on dividends/ salaries	shareholders taxed on profits

ADVANTAGES/DISADVANTAGES OF BUSINESS ENTITIES

	Sole Proprietor	Partnership	Corporation	S-Corp.
ADVANTAGES	• ease of formation • flexible • only taxed once at individual level • ease of operation • centralized management • maximum control	• ease of formation • flexible • only taxed once at individual level • division of labor • increased sources of capital • employee incentives	• separate legal entity • limited liability • continuity of existence • ownership transferable • increased sources of capital • employee incentives • separate ownership/management	• separate legal entity • limited liability • continuity of existence • continuity of management • ownership transferable • increased sources of capital • employee incentives • separate ownership/management
DISADVANTAGES	• unlimited liability • limited sources of capital • no continuity of existence • owner's salary not deductible as expense	• unlimited liability • no centralized management • no continuity of existence • owner's salary not deductible as expense	• difficult formation • expensive formation • government regulation • inflexible • double taxation	• difficult formation • expensive formation • government regulation • inflexible • only one class of stock • only 35 shareholders

BUSINESS FORMS

Certain business forms and contracts introduced into a business structure may also provide a measure of protection for trainers. Contracts between client and trainer can be utilized in a variety of ways (contracts such as informed consents, assumptions of risk and prospective waivers/releases of liability are dealt with separately in Chapter 5). Trainers may want to consider the practicality of using short-term and long-term contracts with their clients. Such contracts bind the client to stay in the program for a specified term, much like some basic health club contracts. However, such contract forms also bind the trainer in providing services to a particular client for a specified time period. Lastly, these contracts also ensure that the client is monetarily committed to the program, thus helping to ensure a certain amount of cash flow for the business over the designated period.

The trainer using long-term or short-term contracts should be aware of the recent legislative trend in many states limiting the duration, methods of payment and other terms of health spa type contracts. Many states now have "Health Spa Acts" which provide for monthly payments rather than full payment in advance, prohibit lifetime contracts, and specify a two or three year limit on the duration of any single health spa contract, *see,* Hawaii Health Spa Act, H.R.S. 486N (Supp. 1989). Such legislation may be applicable to the personal trainer using similar contracts with clients. The specific laws in each jurisdiction must be researched by program counsel before the trainer utilizes short-term or long-term contracts in this regard.

Usually these service contracts will spell out the contract price for services and methods of payment as well as other terms. However, all trainers should develop and use an effective client policy statement which should outline the relationship between the trainer and the client. *See* sample client policy statement in the Appendix.

An effective policy statement should include statements concerning no-shows and cancellations, billing and late payment policy, punctuality, length of training sessions, what forms need to be signed before the program begins and so forth. The trainer might also consider adding requirements that the client commit to an introductory package of workouts as well as maintain a diet log and exercise article folder. The advantage of an effective policy statement is to avoid confusion and misunderstanding down the road. The trainer might also want to consider having the client sign and date the document as an acknowledgment of and agreement to its terms.

The trainer who hires either employees or independent contractors to provide some client services should consider using agreements with these associate trainers. A basic employee/independent contractor agreement outlines the terms of employment and should include the nature of the work to be performed, compensation to be paid, status as an employee or as an independent contractor, as well as a covenant not to compete and/or pirate clients, employees or trade secrets.

A covenant not to compete or pirate certain "trade secrets" or "proprietary information" restricts an employee/independent contractor's ability to solicit both clientele as well as employees for a specified period of time after ceasing employment. This can be a very important tool to use in protecting a trainer's business.

A covenant not to compete may also attempt to limit or altogether prohibit the departing employee/independent contractor from competing in the personal training field against the former employer for a specified time. While the solicitation provisions of the covenant normally will be upheld, covenants not to compete that restrict an employee/independent contractor's ability to compete in the same field in a manner which is unduly restrictive are narrowly construed. In the case of an independent contractor they may not even be upheld. In general, the covenant not to compete language cannot be overly broad or restrictive in terms of geographical restrictions as well as time restrictions. *See,* sample independent contractor/employee agreements in the Appendix.

EMPLOYEES

As was mentioned in Chapter 2, the status of the trainer as an employee or an independent contractor can affect both the potential liability and the tax implications of both the trainer and the club owner/employer. The Internal Revenue Service (I.R.S.) has promulgated various Revenue Rulings outlining what factors the Service takes into consideration in classifying one as either an employee or an independent contractor. While various proposals have recently been put forth to assist in the determination process as to these matters, the general "employee/independent contractor test" encompasses a variety of different criteria, any one of which standing alone may not be dispositive, but when taken together form a basis for classifying a worker as one or the other. *See,* I.R.S. Rev. Rul. 87-41 (1988).

The main factor used to make a determination as to whether a worker is an independent contractor or an employee is the "control test". The important point is whether or not the employer has the ability to control the means and methods by which the trainer accomplishes his/her task. If the employer directs how a trainer instructs, that trainer more than likely will be considered an employee. The trainer who is only required to "get results" and whose program is not under the supervision of the employer would more than likely be classified as an independent contractor.

Other factors that come into play for this classification process include:

(a) **Training** – On the job training usually indicates employee status;

(b) **Continuing Relationship** – Most independent contractors work from job to job. A continuing relationship with the employer could point to an employer/employee relationship;

(c) **Set Hours of Work/Full Time Required** – If the employer sets the hours and/or requires the full time of the worker, this indicates control and employee status;

(d) **Payment by the Hour/Week/Month** – Payment by the hour, week or month rather than by the job or task performed points to an employer/employee relationship;

(e) **Reimbursement For Business/Traveling Expenses** – A worker who is reimbursed for any business and/or traveling expenses generally is considered an employee;

(f) **Working for More Than One Employer** – Working for various firms on different jobs indicates independent contractor status;

(g) **Offering Services to the Public at Large** – The worker offering services to the general public normally will be classified as an independent contractor;

(h) **Profit/Loss Potential** – The worker who can realize either a profit or a loss on a job generally is an independent contractor;

(i) **Furnishing of Facilities/Materials/Tools** – The worker who furnishes his or her own facilities, materials and/or tools is usually classified as an independent contractor.

The I.R.S. has listed some twenty factors in Revenue Ruling 87-4, *supra,* that impact on whether or not a particular worker is an employee or an independent contractor. It must be emphasized that no one factor standing alone will determine the status of a particular worker. In light of this, it would be advisable for the club owner contemplating the hiring of independent contractors to consult with both legal and accounting experts for a further clarification of the "independent contractor/ employee test".

As explained in Chapter 2, the doctrine of respondeat superior normally governs the liability created by the employer/employee relationship. For the most part, an employer will be held responsible for the negligent acts of his/her employees acting within the scope of their employment. An employer can attempt to limit exposure to liability by hiring independent contractors. Generally, the independent contractor/employer relationship is not governed by the doctrine of respondeat superior. The employer who desires to limit his or her liability for the actions of a trainer by hiring an independent contractor must also realize that by doing so, the employer loses the right to control the actions of that trainer.

For the trainer, independent contractor status may give freedom of control in training methods and philosophies, but with that freedom comes responsibility for taxes as well as potential primary and sole liability for negligent acts. Both the trainer and the employer should discuss the pros and cons of employee versus independent contractor status with legal counsel prior to selecting one form of relationship over another.

Lastly, the question of worker's compensation needs to be addressed in this context. For the employee fitness trainer, potential work-related injuries will be covered under the employer's worker's compensation policy. But what of the independent contractor trainer who is injured on the job? Normally, the independent contractor will not be covered under the other party's policy. It is advisable for the freelancing trainer to explore questions of worker's compensation and how to obtain coverage before taking on an independent contractor job. In fact, many clubs may require that trainers provide proof of the requisite insurance coverage, including worker's compensation, liability insurance and health insurance before performance of the contract can even begin.

LIABILITY INSURANCE

Personal trainers and other fitness professionals are now able to procure relatively low premium liability insurance policies through such organizations as ACSM. Many of these policies provide million dollar limits of liability on their insurance coverages. The question remains however, just how far do these policies go in scope of coverage and permitted activities?

Insurance executives caution personal trainers to exercise professional judgment when taking clients outdoors to train. Although many insurance policies for fitness professionals will cover the trainer operating out of a club or in the client's home or office, there are "gray" areas when services are rendered off-site. Not all off-site activities and environments will necessarily fall under the protection of a particular policy.

Trainers are also advised by insurance professionals to stick within the normal confines of exercise, and to avoid teaching dangerous activities in dangerous environments. Certain activities such as mountain climbing, ocean aerobics and the martial arts may not be covered by a typical policy.

Aside from getting clarification on the "gray" areas outlined above, trainers should investigate the scope of coverage available from various insurance underwriters. Depending upon the business' services and needs, a variety of coverages may be necessary and desirable to adequately insure against accidental loss, *see* Herbert, "Recent Developments In The Insurance Industry Affecting Exercise, Rehabilitation And Health Fitness Professionals," *The Exercise Standards and Malpractice Reporter* 2(5):74-75, 1988.

A general liability policy covers the trainer and/or business for acts of general negligence. This policy is usually broad in scope, encompassing most claims brought against a policy holder. Professional liability insurance on the other hand is narrower and primarily covers acts of negligence related to a failure of the trainer to conform his or her behavior to the appropriate professional standard of care. Since some trainers are being taken to court over their alleged lack of professional competence, *see* Rabinoff, "An Examination of Four Recent Cases Against Fitness Instructors," *The Exercise Standards and Malpractice Reporter* 2(3):43-47, 1988, all trainers could benefit from such coverage in event of claim and lawsuit.

Personal injury liability insurance provides for coverage in the event a trainer is sued for defamation of character and injury to one's personal and/or business reputation. Defamation covers both libel (written harm) and slander (spoken harm).

Other insurance to cover certain employment based risks may also be available to cover negligence type actions arising out of the employment relationship. However, such insurance is often costly and will probably not cover unlawful or intentional violations of employment related laws and statutes.

The business owner will want to ensure that he/she not only has the above policies covering employees, but also policies specifically covering the business assets. Property insurance will provide coverage in the event of a loss to the physical plant and/or its equipment and/or contents. Generally, property insurance only protects against losses resulting from fire, smoke, wind, hail, riot and vandalism. Business interruption insurance provides coverage in the event that a property loss results in the interruption of services. Such coverage will usually reimburse the business for lost earnings and profits as well as extra expenses involved in running a business that is destroyed or damaged by one of the calamities mentioned above. For a more comprehensive overview of the various types of insurance available to the fitness professional, *see* Frick, "Insurance Needs," **AEROBIC DANCE-EXERCISE INSTRUCTOR MANUAL**, pp. 357-362 (IDEA Foundation 1987).

The business also needs to insure that both employees and independent contractors are adequately covered by insurance. If an independent contractor does not carry his or her own policy, the business should make sure that the independent contractor is covered under the business policy, perhaps as an additional insured. However, a trainer freelancing as an independent contractor should procure his or her own policy.

FINAL THOUGHT

Tending to the business structure in the initial planning stages of the business can greatly enhance the potential protection from risk of loss and liability. The trainer should not underestimate the importance of the concepts herein discussed, nor should the actions suggested herein be delayed until the business is up and running. The trainer should consult with appropriate professionals early on to ensure that the ground floor of the business is solidly developed before the business actually begins. Attention to business planning is an ongoing and developing process which requires periodic review and evaluation.

Chapter 5

INFORMED CONSENT, PROSPECTIVE RELEASE/ WAIVER AND ASSUMPTION OF RISK DOCUMENTS

Before starting a client on an exercise program, the personal fitness trainer needs to comply with certain legal formalities for the benefit of the client and to provide self protection from potential lawsuits through the use of various program documents. In this regard, informed consent, assumption of the risk, and prospective release/waiver documents need to be drafted by program legal counsel for use by trainers. Although, upon first glance, these documents may appear quite similar, they have very different legal meanings and implications for the one-on-one professional.

In general, an informed consent document basically gives the trainer the client's permission to have the client undergo an exercise test, prescription or activity. The consent is not an informed one unless the client is provided facts and information, and appreciates and understands the material and relevant risks involved with the activity or range of activities to be carried on by the client. A release/waiver on the other hand prospectively releases the trainer from liability for untoward occurrences. An assumption of risk document states that the client has been informed of, appreciates and understands the risks of exercise or activity and assumes any and all risks of injury associated therewith.

INFORMED CONSENT

In the field of fitness, an informed consent document is a voluntary agreement from a client who has been informed of, appreciates, and understands the material and relevant risks associated with participation in the activity or range of activities involved in exercise testing and activity provided through prescription. Under the law, no one is privileged to touch another person without his/her consent to do so. A cause of action for civil or criminal battery may lie for any harmful or offensive contact or touching of a person or object closely associated with that person absent consent – either express or provided by implication of law. In exercise testing and prescription, the client undergoes various physical activities and physiological changes which can be construed as either actual or constructive contact. Therefore, an informed consent is necessary to gain the client's permission to proceed with such contact.

The informed consent process is most commonly found in the field of medicine. It can be considered malpractice if a medical professional undertakes a medical procedure without having first obtained an informed consent from the patient. The need for an informed consent for participation in an exercise program has gained acceptance over the past few years and can now be considered standard practice in the industry. While full compliance with the requirements for informed consent in a medical context is undoubtedly not required for fitness related activities, compliance with the process will adequately inform the client of the activities to be undertaken and the risks associated therewith, while protecting the trainer from claims related to battery, misrepresentation or negligent provision of information.

In order for a client to validly consent to an exercise test/prescription, the following requirements need to be met:

1. the client must be legally capable of giving his/her consent (*i.e.,* of valid age and competent);

2. the client must be fully informed of, know, appreciate and understand the relevant and material risks involved in giving consent (*i.e.,* the consent must be an informed one);

3. the client's consent must be voluntary (*i.e.,* not given under duress or mistake of fact).

See Herbert & Herbert, **LEGAL ASPECTS OF PREVENTIVE, REHABILITATIVE & RECREATIONAL EXERCISE PROGRAMS** (Third Edition) (PRC Publishing, Inc., Canton, Ohio, 1993).

The question remains as to what exactly constitutes an informed consent. The earlier "professional rule" standard which courts used when deciding informed consent questions, allowed a physician a measure of discretion as to what constituted a full disclosure of the risks involved in a proposed procedure to the patient. The argument for allowing physicians to use their professional judgment was that informing the patient of all risks, no matter how minute, could actually be detrimental to the patient by causing the patient undue anxiety and thereby adversely affecting the treatment to be provided to the patient. Thus, the physician was given the discretion to "weed" out remote risks (such as death or stroke) and inform the patient of only those risks that were deemed material, *i.e.,* with a high to moderate chance of occurring. *Id.* at 196-197; *see also* Banja, "Informed Consent: Historical Development And Relevance To Exercise And Cardiac Rehabilitation Programs," *The Exercise Standards and Malpractice Reporter* 3(4):53-60, 1989.

Recent developments in the informed consent disclosure process have called into doubt the measure of discretion afforded physicians. In some jurisdictions the foregoing "professional rule" has been displaced by the "patient's need for information doctrine". Under this doctrine, the informed consent process requires a disclosure of *"all information material to the patient's making a truly informed and intelligent decision concerning the proposed medical procedure." See* Herbert, "Risk Disclosure In The Informed Consent Process: Judging The Adequacy Of Disclosure In Light Of The Patient's Need For Information, An Emerging Trend," *The Exercise Standards and Malpractice Reporter* 2(4):56-57, 1988, *analyzing* Paucher v. Iowa Methodist Medical Center, No. 86-364 (Supreme Court, Iowa, June 17, 1987); "Informed Consent and New Disclosure Responsibilities for Exercise Stress Testing: The Case of Hedgecorth v. United States, *The Exercise Standards and Malpractice Reporter* 1(2):30-32, 1987.

The "patient's need for information doctrine" has potentially serious consequences for the exercise professional. Such changes in the informed consent disclosure process could require exercise professionals to not only disclose "material" risks involved in the exercise program, but remote risks as well. While the occurrence of a serious, debilitating injury, stroke and/or death is extremely remote in both exercise testing and prescribed or recommended activity, the new doctrine could still require disclosure of all the risks associated therewith. Since the "patient's need for information doctrine" has gained acceptance in a growing number of states (at least 16), it may become more widespread in the future. Due to these conflicting doctrines, it is critical that the personal trainer consult with legal counsel who is thoroughly familiar with the informed consent disclosure requirements applicable in a given jurisdiction.

While adherence to a "medical" informed consent process is probably not necessary for exercise programs, compliance with the procedure of informed consent will undoubtedly assist the client in understanding the risks associated with contemplated activity. It will also assist the trainer in protecting him/herself in the event of an untoward occurrence. While informed consent in a medical setting can be a potentially complicated and extensive process depending upon the circumstances and procedure to be performed, the personal fitness trainer should use a much simpler consent form adapted to the setting of personal fitness training. Since undergoing a medical procedure can have serious and far reaching implications for both patient and doctor, the physician is held to a much higher standard than will the fitness trainer in the informed consent process. This is particularly true in the disclosure section of the consent. The physician may have a much more extensive duty to disclose remote risks than the fitness trainer. And while even the safest medical procedures can contain a strong element of risk, the safest activity programs normally contain a very low incidence of risk. However, the simple consent process in the exercise setting should still follow the general guidelines of a "medical" consent.

The following guidelines for administering the informed consent process in an exercise setting may be appropriate:

1. Consent should be obtained in writing, on a pre-printed form, preceded by an explanation of relevant and material risks involved in the exercise program or procedure;

2. Separate forms for exercise testing, rehabilitative programs, and preventive programs should be used;

3. Informed consent for participation in an exercise program should state the purpose of the exercise program;

4. The informed consent form should contain plain layman's language, adequately disclose the risks and benefits involved, provide space for listing questions, answers and comments about the process, be signed and dated by the participant (and/or legal guardian in the case of a minor) and staff member, and provide for a reproduced copy of the consent form to be given to the client;

5. The client's file should be documented with the original of the signed and dated form;

6. The consent should apply so as to allow <u>all</u> staff members to interact with the client;

7. Separate consents for the use of the client's picture, name and other relevant information must be obtained so as to avoid violating the client's right to privacy in the event of use. *See* sample informed consent document in the Appendix.

While the personal fitness trainer should be aware of the benefits of obtaining a valid and defensible informed consent from the client, such a document will not shield the trainer from liability in the event that the trainer acts in a negligent manner and breaches his/her professional duty. Trainers should be aware that, depending upon the circumstances and jurisdiction in question, prospective release/waiver forms might however provide a measure of protection from liability for negligent acts that give rise to client injury.

PROSPECTIVE RELEASE/WAIVER DOCUMENTS

Prospective releases/waivers have been used in the fitness industry for years in an attempt to absolve a facility from liability for member injuries. Facilities have traditionally attempted to limit their liability by having members sign such general disclaimer forms or "liability waivers". Such forms purported to release the facility and its staff from any and all liability associated with any and all injuries or claims of its members, including claims of negligence in advance of any occurrence.

In the past, some courts have looked upon such blanket waivers unfavorably, reasoning that documents which absolve a facility from responsibility for negligence would be against public policy. Yet, there has been a growing tendency of the courts to give affect to such documents where they are properly written, read and understood by the participant and duly executed, *see,* Cotten & Cotten (Eds.), **LEGAL ASPECTS OF WAIVERS IN SPORT, RECREATION AND FITNESS ACTIVITIES** (PRC Publishing, Inc., Canton, OH 1997).

The personal trainer should be aware that the validity of prospective release/waiver forms is peculiar to the circumstances surrounding the incident, as well as the jurisdiction examining the use of each such form. In any event, some general observations can be made from the cases both upholding and striking down prospective releases used in exercise settings. In the first place, a distinction may need be drawn between active negligence (teaching a contraindicated exercise) and passive negligence (failing to keep the exercise area free from potential hazards). In some jurisdictions, passive negligence may be disclaimed under proper circumstances. In other jurisdictions, a trainer may never be able to absolve him/herself from active negligence.

Secondly, prospective releases which unambiguously and explicitly set forth the "range of activities" to which it applies ("injuries while using any and all equipment") have been upheld in some jurisdictions. Other jurisdictions have held such clauses unenforceable whereby the exculpatory language was not couched in clear, concise terms and did not provide for all contingencies ("slip and fall" incidents on facility premises).

Thirdly, releases which do not clearly and explicitly state that the clients are relieving the provider from liability for among other things, negligence, often do not withhold scrutiny. In such circumstances the use of the word "negligence" within the form may be required.

Lastly, release/waiver documents need to be supported by adequate consideration, *i.e.,* something of value, to be upheld. The fitness center or trainer must be giving something, such as services or facility access, to obtain a validly supported waiver/release. Thus, it is important to have such forms signed at the initiation of the program and considered as part of the "purchase price" for the services.

The necessity for clear and concise language in release/waiver documents strongly points to the need to have the law researched and drafted by an experienced attorney in the trainer's jurisdiction. For an example of a prospective release/waiver document, *see,* sample form in the Appendix. Due to the traditional hostility against, and uncertainty concerning some such forms, the trainer may want to consider incorporating assumption of risk language in such forms.

ASSUMPTION OF RISK

In certain circumstances, assumption of risk language, as opposed to release/waiver language, may be appropriate for personal fitness trainer use with clients. For a client to have been said to have voluntarily assumed a risk of injury, the client (1) must be informed of, understand, and appreciate the risks of injury involved with the activity or "range of activities" that he or she is engaging in; and, (2) must be voluntarily proceeding in the face of such risks.

One of the main differences between assumption of risk and informed consent documents is that the former is used as a defense to a negligence action, while the latter is used as a prospective authorization to particular conduct with a client, *see* Herbert, "Express Assumption Of Risk As A Defense To Negligence Claims: A Practical Analysis," *The Exercise Standards and Malpractice Reporter* 1(6):91-96, 1987. For the most part, assumption of risk should be "express" (written), particularly in a comparative negligence jurisdiction. It should also be noted that generally, clients cannot be said to have assumed the risk of injury outside of the normal range of activities involved in an exercise program. For instance, a client cannot be said to have assumed the risk of structural deficiencies in a facility that cause participant injury unless he or she knew of those risks and agreed to proceed with activity despite the condition.

FINAL THOUGHT

The need for implementing appropriate forms into a personal trainer program cannot be underestimated or overemphasized. Likewise, the involvement of experienced and knowledgeable legal counsel in researching the applicable law and in drafting appropriate forms in compliance with that law is critical. In this litigious society one cannot be too cautious in this regard. Of course, along with utilizing appropriate program documents, the best protection against successful suit is ensuring that professional conduct adheres to the highest applicable standards of care.

Chapter 6

HEALTH SCREENING, FITNESS ASSESSMENT AND THE UNAUTHORIZED PRACTICE OF MEDICINE

Pre-activity health screening and fitness assessment should be standard practice for the trainer before starting a new client on an exercise program. Such screening and assessment which now clearly appears to be part of the standard of care required of personal fitness trainers should begin with the completion of a detailed health/medical/fitness history questionnaire (including coronary risk factor identification) by the client. Such questions should then be used to assess a client's fitness level, as well as to differentiate between apparently healthy individuals and those high risk individuals who should be referred to a physician for clearance and further evaluation prior to beginning trainer prescribed activity or fitness program. Such a questionnaire should elicit responses to inquiries concerning the client's past and present medical history, family medical history, past and present fitness/recreation history, and nutritional habits.

The trainer should attempt where appropriate to get the client's personal physician involved in the program through consultations between trainer and physician or client and physician. Although it should be standard practice to refer high risk individuals for physician clearance and further evaluation, it might be prudent to require physician clearance for all clients. The trainer would be wise to suggest that even apparently healthy clients undergo a pre-activity physical and where appropriate, a graded exercise test.

Along with pre-activity screening and assessment, a system of periodic and regular reassessment should also be introduced into the program. With all the above in mind, the personal fitness trainer should take note to avoid making any medical analysis/diagnosis or to suggest treatment for any medical conditions.

HEALTH/FITNESS HISTORY FORMS

Arguably the most important step in the pre-activity health screening and fitness assessment process, the health/medical/fitness history form should become standard practice in each trainer's program. Written health screening/fitness assessment forms should be utilized for two basic purposes: (1) for the personal fitness trainer's determination of a client's "level of fitness" as opposed to "state of health"; and (2) for screening purposes to determine whether the client should be referred to a medical professional for a pre-activity physical/graded exercise stress test and medical clearance. Health screening/fitness assessment forms should never be used to medically diagnose, prescribe, provide, and/or recommend treatment for any medical condition or ailment. The use of these screening tools for such purposes might very well expose the trainer to a claim of the unauthorized practice of medicine or some other allied health profession. Such a claim could also open up the trainer to a higher standard of care in the event of an accident, *see* Herbert, "Appropriate Use of Wellness Appraisals," *Fitness Management* at 23, Sept. 1989; Herbert, "Legal Implications in Health-Screening Use," *Fitness Management* at 19, Dec. 1989.

The health screening/fitness assessment process should include some method of coronary risk factor identification to differentiate between apparently healthy individuals (without known or suspected heart disease) and high risk individuals. Such an analysis can be included within the health/medical/fitness history questionnaire, or a supplemental form such as the **PAR Q** form developed in Canada, can be utilized. An adequate coronary risk factor identification form should contain questions pertaining to the identification of major coronary risk factors as outlined by the ACSM. These include a history of high blood pressure, *e.g.,* above 145/95, elevated total cholesterol or a high density lipoprotein cholesterol ratio (above 5), cigarette smoking, abnormal resting ECG, family history of coronary or other cardiovascular disease prior to age 50, or a history of diabetes mellitus.

An adequate health/medical/fitness history chart should follow the guidelines promulgated by ACSM, and should elicit responses to questions concerning the client's past and present medical history, family medical history, past and present fitness/recreation history, and health/nutritional habits.

The health/fitness history section should contain, among other things, questions related to injuries, exercise habits, use of alcohol, tobacco and caffeine, nutritional habits, and stress. The medical history section of the questionnaire should address the client's past and present medical history, and should elicit information regarding heart disease, diabetes, high/low blood pressure, stroke, etc. (including symptoms relating to the above), as well as past surgery, past and present injuries, drug allergies and past and present medications.

Family medical history information (grandparents, parents, aunts, uncles and siblings) should be explored for heart attack/disease, coronary operations, strokes, high blood pressure, diabetes, and elevated cholesterol. The personal fitness trainer can also address the client's specific fitness goals in the health/medical/fitness history questionnaire, as well as acquire a nutritional profile. For a more detailed checklist as to the areas and questions that should be addressed in the above form, *see,* sample health/fitness questionnaire in the Appendix.

From a professional standpoint, an adequate exercise program cannot be properly designed without the taking of a comprehensive health/medical/fitness history on the client. An exercise professional should not attempt to prescribe exercise without first knowing something about the client's health, medical condition and fitness background. Exercise professionals should know how much a client's past health/medical/fitness history can impact on the type, duration, intensity and frequency of exercise. In the same vein, from a legal standpoint there may be a duty to adequately screen clients prior to the client undertaking an exercise program. In fact, inadequate screening, or no screening at all, could very well expose the client to harm and the trainer to a negligence claim in the event that a past or present health or medical condition contraindicates a particular exercise program, or exercise in general, and injury occurs. *See* Herbert, "Is There A Legally Mandated Duty To Screen Exercise Participants Prior To Exercise?," *The Exercise Standards and Malpractice Reporter: Lawyer's Edition* 1(2):22-24, September, 1987.

PHYSICIAN INVOLVEMENT

The trainer should attempt when appropriate to get the client's personal physician involved in the program through regular consultations. If the above health/medical/fitness history form and risk factor identification questionnaire indicates that a particular candidate is a high risk individual, that individual should be referred to a physician for further screening, evaluation and medical clearance before beginning the trainer's exercise program and at periodic intervals during the program. The trainer should never attempt to further evaluate a high risk candidate, or start the client on an exercise program, once risk factors have been identified, without requiring medical clearance.

Although it should be standard practice to refer high risk individuals for physician clearance and further screening and evaluation, it might be prudent, as previously stated, to require physician clearance for all clients. *See* sample physician approval form in the Appendix. The trainer would be wise to suggest that even apparently healthy clients undergo a pre-activity physical and physician supervised graded exercise test prior to beginning any type of exercise program. This is particularly true for older, sedentary individuals who may nonetheless be classified as apparently healthy.

Risk factor identification should not be the only criteria that activates consultation with the client's physician. The physician should be questioned regarding medications currently prescribed and their effect on exercise, drug allergies, past surgeries, and the effects of any past and/or present injuries and limited ranges of motion, as well as the client's overall general health. These consultations should take place before the client begins his/her program, and should be documented by detailed, written notes. The initial consultation with the client's physician can be immediately followed up with a written physician approval form which secures the physician's signed approval for the client to participate in the trainer's program, listing any restrictions that apply.

Lastly, physician consultation should be an ongoing part of the client's program, particularly during the trainer's periodic and regular reassessment of clients. The client's physician should also be contacted after every client physical and office visit for further consultation. The relationship should be a two-way street, with the trainer reporting to the physician on the client's level of fitness while the physician can update the trainer on the client's present (and past) state of health or for recommended modifications to the prescribed program. Appropriate releases for information to be provided by the physician should be secured from the patient so that the physician may supply information to the personal fitness trainer, *see* sample form in the Appendix.

EXERCISE TESTING

ACSM's **GUIDELINES FOR EXERCISE TESTING AND PRESCRIPTION** position concerning exercise testing differs according to the age and health status of the individual. Pursuant to these **GUIDELINES**, apparently healthy individuals (those individuals without any major coronary risk factors and free from disease) under the age of 45 usually can begin a gradual exercise program without the need for exercise testing, while those apparently healthy individuals above the age of 45 should undergo a maximal exercise test prior to beginning an exercise program. For those clients at a high risk (having at least one major coronary risk factor) and/or with suspected disease, exercise testing is desirable, while those clients with known disease should undergo exercise testing.

The ACSM **GUIDELINES** further state that physician supervision of maximal testing is recommended in all cases except for apparently healthy individuals under the age of 35. Submaximal testing can be performed without physician supervision in the case of all apparently healthy individuals, and for those high risk individuals under the age of 35 who have no symptoms of cardiopulmonary or metabolic disease. In the case of those high risk individuals over 35 and/or with symptoms, physician attendance is recommended before submaximal testing.

Although guidelines such as those promulgated by ACSM and other organizations such as the AHA, contain rather clear-cut recommendations regarding supervision and administration of exercise tests, controversy still remains as to just who can (and who should) legally supervise and administer exercise tests. Is it the physician, nurse, physical therapist, or exercise physiologist? And under what circumstances can all or some of the above partake in the procedure? *See* Herbert, "Is Physician Supervision of Exercise Stress Testing Required?," *The Exercise Standards and Malpractice Reporter* 2(1):6-7, January 1988.

One health practitioner who advocates supervision of clinical exercise tests by highly trained nurses believes that policies concerning physician supervision of graded exercise tests have a stronger legal/historical basis than one grounded in medical procedure, *see* DeBusk, "Exercise Test Supervision: Time For Reassessment," *The Exercise Standards and Malpractice Reporter* 2(5): 65, Oct/Nov. 1988. Yet, according to one legal commentator, *"[f]rom a legal standpoint it appears quite clear that there is a greater litigation risk associated with procedures which are carried out without direct physician supervision, especially if such procedures are clearly medical in nature. Even in situations where there is an appropriate and legally defensible delegation of responsibility for administration and/or supervision to a non-physician, the physician should regularly examine the procedures, personnel and protocols and maintain overall supervisory knowledge of patient care and the course of treatment."* *See* Herbert, "Is Physician Supervision of Exercise Stress Testing Required?," *The Exercise Standards and Malpractice Reporter* 2(1):6, January 1988. For a more extensive discourse on why physician supervision of exercise tests for individuals with known cardiovascular disease is necessary, *see* Gibbons, "Who Should Supervise An Exercise Test,"

The Exercise Standards and Malpractice Reporter 3(6):85-91, Oct./Nov. 1989.

There is also some thought that graded exercise tests should be standard procedure to screen all men who wish to begin activity who are over the age of 40 for silent ischemia. This opinion appears to result from a California case which resulted in a $500,000 arbitration award for the family of a man who died of a heart attack at the age of 40. The man who desired to commence an activity program had undergone a physical without a stress test which failed to disclose the presence of silent ischemia. He was released without further evaluation, and without restriction on activity, and was scheduled for a follow-up visit several months later. Thereafter while jogging, he suffered a myocardial infarction and subsequently died. *See* Herbert, "Are GXTs Required of All Men Over 40?," *The Exercise Standards and Malpractice Reporter* 2(2):30, April 1988.

The personal fitness trainer should also be aware that while certain national standards relating to exercise testing have been promulgated by a number of organizations such as ACSM, different states have adopted their own standards either through legislation or standard setting organizations such as State Boards of Medical Examiners. In North Carolina, for example, according to a June, 1987 statement of the State Board of Medical Examiners, the standard for administration of GXTs is *"that a physician is in the room or immediate area." See* Trends, "Physician Must Be Present For Administration of Graded Exercise Tests," *The Exercise Standards and Malpractice Reporter* 1:75, 1987.

With the divergence of opinion regarding exercise testing, the personal fitness trainer who contemplates conducting exercise testing him or herself should consult with legal counsel regarding the effect of state laws and standards upon such a contemplated procedure. In the absence of any state guidelines, the trainer should take a conservative approach to administering and supervising exercise testing. At a minimum, the trainer should follow the guidelines developed by the ACSM. To play it safe, maximal testing should always be administered by a physician, while submaximal testing may have to be supervised by a physician.

THE UNAUTHORIZED PRACTICE OF MEDICINE

As was intimated earlier in this chapter, health screening, fitness assessment, and exercise programming are areas in which the personal fitness trainer has to be cautious not to cross over into the practice of medicine or some allied health profession. The practice of medicine is usually defined by state statute and written rather broadly. While the unauthorized practice of medicine may be contained in such definitions by implication, some states go as far as to explicitly define what in fact constitutes the unauthorized practice of medicine. In any event, the professional should become thoroughly familiar with his/her state's statutory definition of the practice of medicine and other licensed/regulated allied health care disciplines. Consultation with program counsel regarding the legal implications of such statutes as applied to the personal fitness trainer's program is also advisable.

The potential problems that a personal fitness trainer might experience as to a claim related to the unauthorized practice of medicine or some allied health profession begins with the health/medical/fitness questionnaire. As was mentioned above, the professional should remember that one of the main purposes of health screening/fitness assessment is to determine the client's "level of fitness". The personal fitness trainer must avoid rendering any medical analysis/diagnosis/opinion relating to the client's "state of health," or to suggest treatment for any medical conditions based upon a reading or assessment of such screening devices. Such medically related actions could open the personal fitness trainer up to a claim of the unauthorized practice of medicine or other allied health care discipline, as well as possibly elevating the expected standard of care to that of one providing health care services.

A second area particularly vulnerable to a claim of the unauthorized practice of medicine is fitness testing. With all the controversy surrounding who can legally, ethically and professionally administer and/or supervise exercise testing, the trainer should tread lightly to ensure that he/she is not violating any state statutes or state mandated practices or procedures regarding such matters. The personal fitness trainer may find himself or herself in a catch-22 regarding exercise testing; on the one hand, exercise testing can be utilized to determine a client's "level of fitness" and readiness for a particular exercise program. At the same time, that same exercise test may very well give the personal fitness trainer information regarding a client's "state of health," such as disclosing silent ischemia and related heart disease.

In one vein some are suggesting that trainers can administer exercise tests in certain circumstances without physician supervision, and may even have a duty to screen all men over the age of 40 for silent ischemia. *See* Herbert, "Are GXTs Required of All Men Over 40?," *The Exercise Standards and Malpractice Reporter* 2(2):30, April, 1988. In another vein state statutes concerning the practice of medicine may prohibit such screening by non-physicians, particularly if the contemplated procedures are "medically" related. Due to such ambiguities, the professional needs to consult legal counsel and become thoroughly familiar with the state laws in his/her jurisdiction pertaining to exercise testing and the unauthorized practice of medicine or some allied health profession.

Exercise programming could also violate state statutes regarding the practice of medicine if the personal fitness trainer designs a program as treatment for a medical condition, or even suggests certain exercises to improve known health problems. *See,* Stetina v. State Medical Licensing Board, 513 N.E. 2d 1234 (Indiana App. 2 Dist. 1987). Exercise programming should be designed by the fitness professional with the goal of improving the client's fitness as opposed to health. The personal fitness trainer should refrain from making any claims or statements relating to the impact of exercise on one's state of health. The personal fitness trainer should also refrain from using such terminology as exercise prescription with clients, which may have medical connotations. The term "exercise programming" should be utilized instead.

Dieting advice can also expose the personal fitness trainer to an unauthorized practice of medicine claim:

"Even the prescription or recommendation of mineral waters, vitamins or food, under certain circumstances, may be deemed to be prescription for medical purposes, akin to the prescription of drugs, so as to bring such practices within the broad definition of the practice of medicine. The key to these determinations centers upon whether or not the prescription or recommendation is made, dispensed or given to treat, cure or even prevent some disease or condition."

See, Herbert & Herbert (Eds.) **LEGAL ASPECTS OF PREVENTIVE, REHABILITATIVE & RECREATIONAL EXERCISE PROGRAMS**, *supra,* at p. 132; Herbert, "Dieting Advice Can Lead To Litigation," *Fitness Management* at 42, January 1990; Herbert, "Are Nutritionists Engaged In The Unauthorized Practice of Medicine?," *The Exercise Standards and Malpractice Reporter* 2(5):76-78, Oct./Nov. 1988.

The personal fitness trainer who is questioned by his/her clients regarding dieting and nutrition may wish to refrain from prescribing or recommending any type of diet or nutritional plan, even if the sole purpose is to facilitate weight loss in an apparently healthy person. The professional would be prudent to limit his/her nutritional counseling to educating the client on common sense nutritional aspects. Counsel again may need to be consulted as to applicability of particular state cases and law on this topic, as the law varies from state to state.

In some states, such as the state of Mississippi, personal fitness trainers may be prohibited from using the title "trainer" to describe their profession or activities. In Mississippi, and perhaps other states, the use of the term "trainer" has been limited by statute and related state interpretation to licensed athletic trainers. The existence of such statements and interpretations will again have to be examined by legal counsel for determination.

FINAL THOUGHT

Health screening, fitness assessment, exercise testing, and exercise programming are all important and vital components of any fitness program. They are also the areas which are most likely to leave the trainer legally vulnerable if the trainer's conduct falls below accepted standards. With the potential for crossovers from certain "fitness" procedures to "medical" procedures, the above areas might also expose the trainer to unauthorized practice of medicine type claims. The trainer needs to be cautioned to take a conservative approach when addressing these areas of the program.

Chapter 7

EQUIPMENT AND FACILITIES

It can safely be said that many of the accidents that occur to fitness participants are due in part to deficiencies in equipment and/or facilities or are associated with the use of such items. Negligently maintained equipment and/or facilities can cause a multitude of problems for the user and the personal fitness trainer alike. For instance, a number of unique legal questions come into play when a trainer engages in his/her trade in a variety of settings utilizing a wide range of equipment. The personal trainer can turn any area into a "fitness facility" and use a wide range of props as "exercise equipment" including those which are not designed, manufactured or provided for that use. Yet, turning a client's spare bedroom into an aerobics room may sound like a good idea until that client injures his/her ankle due to the stress of jumping up or down on an inappropriate floor surface. Also, it may seem like a good idea to incorporate a dining room chair into step-ups until the client slips and falls from it. The prudent course would be for the personal fitness trainer to utilize only safe, reliable and appropriate equipment and facilities available under the circumstances.

FACILITIES

The personal fitness trainer typically utilizes a wide variety of settings for training, be it a fitness facility, the client's home or office, or the outdoors. Each particular setting offers unique challenges to the professional, as well as posing separate and distinct legal questions and potential problems. But before the various legalities of different exercise settings are examined, the client who uses these facilities must be classified under the law of premises liability.

According to this broad area of law, one who is on another's land can be classified as either a trespasser, a licensee or a business invitee. A **TRESPASSER** is one who is on the land (or in a building) of another without the knowledge or permission of the landowner/occupier, and is owed no duty other than to require that the landowner/occupier refrain from intentional acts that could injure the trespasser. A **LICENSEE** is one who is on the land (or in a building) of another with the permission of the landowner/occupier but for the licensee's benefit. The landowner/occupier owes a licensee the duty to protect and warn against known dangers, but does not have a duty to inspect the premises to protect and/or warn against dangers which are unknown to the licensee. A **BUSINESS INVITEE** is one on the landowner/occupier's premises for the express benefit of the owner/occupier, and is owed the highest duty under the law. With a "business invitee" client, the personal fitness trainer would have a duty to inspect the site of activity beforehand and either correct any dangerous conditions or warn of those dangers which a reasonable inspection would disclose. Although there usually is no duty to warn of obvious dangers, the potentially higher duty of the personal fitness trainer may give rise to a duty to warn of almost all dangers as well.

Under these broad general rules, a client being trained in a professional's private exercise studio would more than likely be classified as a "business invitee" who is on the premises for the express benefit of the personal fitness trainer, *i.e.,* for the monetary benefit of the professional. This may even be true where the personal fitness trainer instructs or leads a client in activity in the clients' premises or in other locations as well.

What about the personal fitness trainer who freelances out of someone else's fitness facility? It is fairly clear that in the case where such a trainer is an employee of a club, or other similar facility, the client would be classified as a business invitee of the club and absent an agreement to the contrary, perhaps the personal fitness trainer as well. While the club may owe the primary duty to the client, a non-employee, freelancing personal fitness trainer may owe a duty as well. Thus, in the case of a trainer acting as an independent contractor working out of a club, the trainer might be said to have stepped into the shoes of the clubowner. Under these circumstances, it would be the freelancing trainer who might owe a higher duty to the business invitee client even though the club might also owe such a duty.

And what of the trainer who trains clients in their homes and offices? What duty is owed in these circumstances? Of course the trainer would not be considered the owner of the land, but he/she might very well be considered the occupier. But what of the client, is he or she considered a business invitee in his/her own home?

Due to the uncertainties concerning what duty is owed in what particular setting, the prudent course for the trainer might be to treat his/her client as a business invitee in all circumstances and extend the highest duty of care. This may be the most appropriate action in any case, because during the time that the personal trainer is with the client in the client's premises, the trainer is prescribing and supervising activity. It would be likely to have the use of client premises viewed as part of the trainer's business so as to make the premises constructively the trainer's during such use. Despite the foregoing, the trainer should pay particular attention to the workout area, physically inspecting it for known and unknown dangers before each and every workout. Any dangerous conditions that can be remedied should be immediately undertaken by the trainer. For conditions that cannot be readily corrected, warnings should be clearly given.

Warning signs/notices or similar devices should also be utilized where practical, particularly around wet areas and on or adjacent to exercise equipment. The floors should be kept clear of weights and other objects that could be tripped over or slipped upon. The floors in the weight room and aerobic room should adhere to the highest industry standards and should also be inspected for wear and tear. The trainer should be aware that many accidents in facilities are of the "slip and fall" type which occur due to negligently maintained floors that are either wet, overly slippery, dirty, etc.

Facility inspections should be incorporated into a trainer's policies and procedures. Such inspections should follow a regular and periodic timetable and should include regular maintenance and/or repair of the physical plant and equipment.

The personal fitness trainer has also helped take fitness out of the traditional health club environment and into a variety of unique settings, such as the outdoors. A number of different legal questions and concerns come into play when the trainer provides services off-site and away from a controlled environment. Due to the unique nature of the one-on-one relationship, the trainer may be judged to be an expert in his or her field, and held to a higher standard of care than a typical health club attendant. By combining this higher standard of care with the uncontrolled workout atmosphere presented by the outdoors, a host of potential legal problems and claims may arise.

One such distinct legal concern presented by outdoor training is a trainer's duty to inspect the workout setting and correct or warn of any known or unknown dangers. The law of premises liability or a legal theory based upon such a concept might apply to the provision of services off-site just like it would apply to an exercise facility. A client being trained outdoors may very well be classified as a "business invitee" who is on the occupier's or owner's premises for the express benefit of the owner/occupier. The trainer him or herself would more than likely be considered under such circumstances to be an occupier of the land.

It may not be enough to simply warn of any dangers that a reasonable inspection discloses and that cannot be corrected. Even if the client is fully informed of the dangers and acknowledges an appreciation and understanding of the risks involved, the trainer/occupier may have a secondary duty to provide protection if he or she suspects or has reason to suspect that the client may be injured. An example might be mountain biking in the woods with a client. A warning of potential dangers alone may not suffice. A trainer may have a further duty to provide adequate and proper instruction on the rudiments of safe mountain biking. The trainer may also have a duty to ensure that the client is protected by the proper equipment (helmet, shoes, etc.) and that the bike is in good working order and free from any hazards or dangerous conditions. Appropriate warnings about exercising in particular climates and weather conditions may also need to be given.

The trainer must also carry on any activity on the premises with reasonable care and refrain from any dangerous activities. In the above mountain biking scenario, it may be deemed negligent on the part of the trainer to attempt to traverse a particularly dangerous part of the course that neither the trainer nor the client is familiar with, or that is beyond the skill level of the participant.

Whether training a client outdoors, in the client's home, or at the gym, it should also be kept in mind that while a session is in progress, it is the trainer rather than the client who has the duty to be alert for further anticipated and unanticipated dangers that might arise. The "business invitee" client has the right to expect that the premises have been inspected and are reasonably safe for contemplated use and activity. The client also has the right to rely on the trainer's actual inspection and/or warnings.

Failure to inspect the premises beforehand would in all probability involve negligence on the trainer's behalf.

This is particularly true in the event that a client is injured due to a dangerous condition that a reasonable inspection would have disclosed. Failure to warn of and/or correct any dangerous conditions which a reasonable inspection would disclose and which results in injury to the client or which are known but not corrected nor the subject of appropriate warnings, may be deemed willful and wanton negligence on the part of the trainer. *See* Jacobsen v. Holiday Health Club, Civil Action No. A85, V 1249 (Arapaho County, Colo. 1988), *analyzed in* Herbert, "Failure to Warn/Correct Judged 'Willful & Wanton,'" *Fitness Management* 22, November, 1989, and Rabinoff, "An Examination of Four Recent Cases Against Fitness Instructors," *The Exercise Standards and Malpractice Reporter* 2(3):45-47, 1988. Willful and wanton negligence could subject the trainer to punitive damages over and above those damages awarded for ordinary negligence. Such damages are very rarely, if ever, covered by liability insurance coverages.

The trainer who utilizes a variety of training settings will need to adequately document the inspection, maintenance, repair and warning procedures used in the course of providing service in those settings. Trainers would benefit from consulting with program counsel on developing appropriate policies and procedures dealing with the inspection, maintenance, repair, warning and documentation process in all such settings. The person performing these functions should be required to complete and initial a log pertaining to the function performed, be it an inspection, repair, or basic maintenance. *See* "Equipment and Facilities Log" section, *infra,* in Chapter 9 dealing with documentation. Program counsel should also be consulted regarding the development of appropriate informed consents, prospective releases, and other related program documents pertaining to the provision of services off-site. *See generally* Herbert, "Legal Aspects of Fitness Premises Liability," *Fitness Management* 17, September, 1988.

Lastly, emergency response protocols must be developed and implemented in advance of service delivery to deal with the occurrence of accidents and emergencies during the rendition of personal training services both on-site and outdoors. Such procedures must include current CPR certification and first aid training, as well as knowledge of and planned access to the nearest emergency medical facilities and emergency response team. The trainer or program should develop such protocols with the advice of program counsel, emergency response professionals, and perhaps government and city officials. These programs need to be regularly rehearsed and modified as necessary to insure emergency response preparedness.

EQUIPMENT

Almost everyone who is a serious fitness enthusiast has suffered some sort of equipment related injury in his or her lifetime. Most of these "injuries" are relatively minor involving strained or pulled muscles which sometimes can be attributed to the person's own negligence, *i.e.,* performing an exercise improperly on an exercise machine. Yet more serious and debilitating injuries involving exercise equipment have occurred resulting in significant claims and litigation. For example, a verdict for the plaintiff was rendered in a case in which an exercise bike seat post came through the seat and impaled the user causing severe injuries; *see* Restaino

v. Montgomery Ward & Co., 540 N. E. 2d 797 (Ill. App. 1 Dist. 1989). For a more extensive review of equipment-related injuries, *see* Herbert and Herbert, "Frequent Claims and Suits in Equipment-Related Injuries," *Fitness Management* 22, February 1988. With the client now relying more and more on the personal fitness trainer's judgment concerning equipment choices and purchases, as well as use, the potential for more serious injuries (as well as claims and suits) exists if the proper policies and procedures regarding equipment are neglected or if improper advice is given.

The above-mentioned duty to inspect, maintain, repair and correct or warn against potential known and unknown dangers applies to exercise equipment as well as facilities. Daily (or more frequent) inspections of equipment should be incorporated into all personal fitness trainer activities. Particular attention should be given to cables, pulleys, seats and other moveable and adjustable parts. Nuts and bolts should be examined and tightened if necessary and equipment should be checked for wear and/or abuse. Frayed or worn parts should be immediately repaired or replaced. If a piece of equipment cannot be adequately repaired on the spot, it should be taken out of use until repairs can be completed.

As mentioned earlier in this chapter, the same principals and standards of care regarding inspection, maintenance and repair of equipment and facilities apply no matter what the setting. Usually for the home/office setting the equipment is minimal and can be inspected before every workout and within a matter of minutes. Workout times need not even be challenged by such cautionary procedures. For example, after a run down of a bicycle ergometer and then while the client is using the bicycle ergometer, a personal fitness trainer will have time to inspect the single stack weight machine. Since the equipment is not handling the volume of people that a typical club does, weekly maintenance might even replace daily maintenance. In fact, a client can be set up to do his/her own weekly maintenance log. The log should be checked regularly by the trainer to ensure that the job was done. It should be remembered to discontinue the use of any broken or worn-out equipment until such items can be repaired.

It is very easy to get so caught up in a training program that daily and weekly detail work such as inspections and maintenance/repairs of equipment and facilities are overlooked. But it should be kept in mind that equipment breaks down and wears out even with the most careful attention. Also, there is a need to document such proper procedures in the event that a trainer's actions are ever questioned in a court of law. This point will be further discussed in Chapter 9 dealing with documentation.

Although most equipment related injuries occur due to negligently maintained and/or repaired equipment, the trainer also opens himself/herself up to potential liabilities by selecting and recommending equipment. First of all, by recommending equipment, the client is relying on the trainer's breadth of knowledge and perceived "expertise" in the exercise equipment field. For instance, if a trainer has limited knowledge of equipment and he/she makes a negligent recommendation (the equipment suggested is dangerously defective or inferior according to industry standards) and the client is injured due to that negligent recommendation, the trainer could very well be held liable. Also if there is a failure to either inspect the equipment beforehand or a failure to uncover a design or manufacturing defect that a reasonable inspection would disclose, a trainer could be held liable in the event that a client is injured. If a trainer sells the equipment or receives a commission from a seller for certain recommendations, trainers can also become involved in products liability claims related to such equipment if it is recommended or sold and causes harm.

Trainers who branch out into exercise equipment consulting need to become thoroughly knowledgeable about the equipment they recommend. The trainer should thoroughly test particular models and become knowledgeable as to the literature and specifications on each piece of equipment as well as industry tests and reports. Particular attention should be given to manufacturer's instructions, warnings, and maintenance recommendations. The client should be adequately advised of the potential dangers involved in using each piece of equipment. The manufacturer's warranty should also be studied for the breadth of coverage provided by the warranty. It should also be remembered that misuse or modification of equipment or failure to follow maintenance schedules as to such equipment may void the manufacturer's warranty. As an equipment consultant, trainers should also become knowledgeable as to competing products and be able to document and substantiate why one piece of equipment was recommended over a competitor's brand.

If a client decides to purchase equipment that has been recommended by a trainer, a factory representative if possible should deliver and assemble/install the equipment if installation is required. If the equipment is such that it requires self-assembly, such as a basic weight bench, the trainer should advise the client to follow the manufacturer's instructions. If a trainer assembles the equipment, the manufacturer's instructions must be followed. All warning/instructional stickers must be properly and correctly placed upon the equipment if such is supplied by the manufacturer. Any instructional charts should be clearly visible to the clients. All bolts, nuts and screws should be properly tightened and all parts and accessories should be properly affixed. The client should be advised as to any weight or similar restrictions that apply to the equipment. It should always be remembered that a failure to follow the manufacturer's instructions not only opens up potential legal liabilities, but that such a failure may also void the manufacturer's warranty.

Lastly, it is advisable to skip makeshift equipment for clients and to stick with the highest quality equipment on the market. While improvisation may make a personal trainer unique from other fitness professionals, caution should be exercised with such devices. When it comes to the more advanced and dangerous exercises that require some sophisticated equipment, improvisation should be stopped entirely and state of the art equipment should be used.

FINAL THOUGHT

It cannot be overemphasized that many if not most accidents associated with a trainer's activities occur due in part to deficiencies in equipment and/or facilities. It is therefore wise for the trainer to pay particular attention to the exercise setting and equipment being used during workouts. The use of a little common sense and the incorporation of protective policies and procedures will protect the client from potential accidents and the trainer from claim and suit.

Chapter 8

SUPERVISION AND INSTRUCTION OF CLIENTELE

The nature of the personal fitness training relationship requires that the one-on-one professional be responsible for the supervision and instruction of the individual client's program. Chances are that the personal fitness trainer who individually and exclusively oversees a client's program will be held to a higher standard of care than a typical health club floor staff member *cf.,* Shields v. Stay-Fit Inc., 903 P.2d 525 (Wa.App. Div. 3 1994) *reviewed in* Herbert, "Health Club Release Upheld in the State of Washington," *Fitness Management* 36 (May 1997). That standard of care will require that the professional conform his or her conduct to that which a reasonably prudent personal fitness trainer would perform under like circumstances. The professional should therefore ensure that he/she is providing the requisite supervision and instruction expected of a personal fitness trainer.

SUPERVISION

Supervision of the exercise program should be "specific" and "individualized" and should adhere to the standard of "adequate" and "proper". Adequate supervision refers to the amount of supervision given before, during, and even after exercise. *See* Stotlar, "Legal Guidelines and Professional Responsibilities," **PER-**

SONAL TRAINER MANUAL (ACE, San Diego, CA 1996) at 457. In the case of a personal fitness trainer, that supervision should include paying close and continuous attention in immediate proximity to the client.The trainer should also closely monitor the client's vital signs (such as heart-rate) and perceived exertion, and provide continuous spotting throughout exercise. While a group aerobics class can be taught by an instructor at one end of the room, a trainer who instructs a client in weight training without being in close proximity with that person would not be providing adequate supervision nor would he/she be in an appropriate position to coach, instruct or "spot" the client as the need arises.

Proper supervision pertains to the factual accuracy or correctness of the supervision, *Id.* Proper attention should be given to correct exercise technique, form, and body mechanics. Safe and effective spotting should be provided throughout exercise, even for the most experienced clients.This is particularly true for such potentially hazardous activities as weight training.

Supervision also includes creating a reasonably safe place to train, be it in a home, a client's office, a fitness facility, or even in the the outdoors. The previous chapter pertaining to premises liability and inspection of both facilities and equipment is applicable to ensuring that the overall program is adequately and properly supervised. Ensuring that the client conform his/her conduct to specified safety protocols is also a must. This could include requirements that the client wear appropriate clothes, shoes and related protective gear such as a weight belt and gloves for weight training.

Even in the event that a professional has conformed his or her conduct to the applicable standard by providing adequate and proper supervision, accidents and other untoward events can and do still occur. Adequate and proper supervision requires that the professional be able to respond to such emergencies. Emergency response protocols need to be developed in advance to provide for such untoward occurrences. Written policies and procedures should be developed in advance to include emergency response protocols. This should include CPR and first aid training for all personal trainers, coordinating the policies and procedures with local emergency response teams, police and government officials, as well as holding regular emergency response drills for staff members. Such procedures need to be developed **and** rehearsed. While at least one recent survey would indicate that many health and fitness facilities do not engage in such processes, personal fitness trainers must do so to properly adhere to the applicable standard of care, *see* McInnis et al., "Cardiovascular Screening and Emergency Procedures at Health Clubs and Fitness Centers," *The American Journal of Cardiology* 80:382-383, August, 1997.

Since the one-to-one trainer typically instructs only one client at a time, supervisory policies should include restricting the workout area to only the person being trained, if practical. This is particularly true in the home where young children could inadvertently wander into the workout area and be injured.

INSTRUCTION

The same standard of "adequate" and "proper" applies to instruction as well. Adequate instruction pertains to the amount of instruction and directions given before, during and after exercise, *Id.* at 437. In this regard, questions which might be asked include: Did the trainer adequately instruct the client on the correct form and handling of the weights, both during execution of the exercise and when returning the weight to the floor or rack?

Proper instruction refers to the factual accuracy or correctness of the instruction and directions, *Id.* The relevant questions amount to: Is the trainer following proper industry standards of care and acting as a reasonable trainer would under like circumstances? Is the trainer avoiding contraindicated exercises?

The standards of care in the industry are especially important to the instructional phase involved in personal fitness training. It is here where degree status, certification and continuing education, along with experience play a critical part. Adequate and proper instruction will more than likely be judged upon such standards. It may not necessarily be enough to say that one has a degree or certification. In an ever changing industry, what one does after attaining a minimum level of competency is at times more relevant than the actual attainment of that minimum standard. Continuing education, active involvement in industry organizations, staying current with the latest trade journals and research, attending conventions, participating in lectures and workshops, writing in areas of expertise, etc., are all important in ensuring that the trainer is providing adequate and proper instruction.

But as to what areas do personal fitness trainers actually provide instruction? And does the standard as to such matters vary from activity to activity? Personal fitness trainers run the gamut from being aerobic instructors, weight trainers, strength and conditioning coaches, athletic trainers, physical therapists, massage therapists, aquatic exercise instructors, body builders, martial arts experts – the list goes on and on. Trainers walk with their clients, lift weights with them, run with them, swim with them and spar with them. In short, the personal fitness trainer basically provides instruction as to any exercise program that the client wants or needs and that the trainer is qualified to pursue.

The big difference between a personal fitness trainer and a health club floor staff professional is that the personal trainer's main job and goal is to achieve very specific results with one individual, while the health club floor staff basically oversees the general programs of all the club's members who may be working out at any given time. For instance, the personal fitness trainer is paid to adequately and properly instruct the given activity and supervise the specific program for a particular client all throughout the program. If the trainer fails to adequately supervise a previously instructed activity, say an incline dumbbell press for the chest, and the client injures himself or herself by dropping the weight on his or her foot due to inadequate training or supervision, the trainer may be liable.

But, if a health club attendant properly instructs a member on a piece of exercise equipment, and the member comes back the next day and injures himself or herself on that same piece of equipment due to improper form or execution, the health club attendant more than likely would not be held liable. Why? Because the health club attendant's job was not to individually supervise this member's program. In a basic health club situation that does not provide personal training for each and every member, the health club usually is just offering facilities to its members to utilize at their own risk, as well as only the most basic and general instruction for the total membership. This usually involves the attendant taking each member through a basic orientation of the exercise equipment at the beginning of the person's membership. Even though claims and suits can arise out of such activities (or the alleged lack thereof) (*see, e.g.,* Reeder v. Bally's Total Fitness, Corp., 963 F.Supp. 530 (E.D. Va. 1997) the standard of care as to such activities will probably be different for personal fitness trainers.

The personal fitness trainer's standard pertaining to supervision and instruction really does not change from activity to activity. It is basically the same for the aerobics instructor training a client on a one on one basis as it is for the karate instructor teaching a roundhouse kick. It is an ongoing and very closely monitored process.

While the standard may be the same no mater what activity is being taught, the standard is not necessarily the same from client to client. Different client populations may require adherence to slightly different standards. To illustrate this point, consider a pregnant woman who wants a program that she can safely follow throughout her pregnancy. The supervision standard would definitely be a much higher standard than that involving a healthy and robust 18 year old high school athlete. Of course, constant communication and interaction with the client's doctor would be a must for the perfect women's program. Particular and specialized standards for such activities will have to be followed. The American College of Obstetricians and Gynecologists for example, has developed standards for exercise activity by pregnant exercisers which must be followed. In other situations, with another client, *e.g.,* a recent heart attack victim who has just undergone a triple bypass, the supervision standard would again be an elevated one for this client. Also, the instruction standard would dictate a much slower initiation and progression for this client's program.

Children would also be instructed differently from adults. Because a child is still growing and developing physically, the stress of weight bearing exercises may be contraindicated. The same is true for a 54 year old woman with osteoporosis.

So, while the activity may not necessarily dictate the supervision and instruction standard for the personal trainer, the specific client involved in activity may require different and more intense instructions and supervision according to different standards and guidelines. This is why it is so important for the trainer to establish a good relationship and open lines of communication with the client's physician, when that client is in a client class delineating such interaction.

FINAL THOUGHT

As may be evident from the above, "adequate" and "proper" supervision and instruction is a different standard for the personal fitness trainer than it is for a typical health club attendant. It is rather important that the personal fitness trainer, as well as other fitness professionals, recognize the obvious and not so obvious differences in this standard as applied to them.The proximity of the fitness professional to the client during exercise is one such obvious distinction.

Chapter 9

DOCUMENTATION AND RECORDKEEPING

The preceding chapters have touched upon the need for the personal fitness trainer to put things in writing. The necessity to be thorough in documentation and recordkeeping is two-fold; first of all, written documentation of the client's program provides a much more reliable form of evidence than oral testimony in the event of a lawsuit. Provided that the trainer followed all applicable standards of care and protocols, and provided that the trainer's documentation is thorough and complete and adequately reflects that the trainer followed the standards, such written records can be used in a court of law as "proof" that the trainer did in fact follow and observe the applicable standards of care.

Secondly, such written documentation creates an image of professionalism, and helps the trainer provide updated and complete services to his or her clientele. A trainer who is thorough, complete and accurate in his/her recordkeeping can respond to the necessity for modifications in the program in a more timely fashion than the trainer who does not keep adequate records. Records and reasonably accurate documentation can also preserve in written form what happens during training when memories will fail in recalling what happened at times which may be distant and far removed from the testimony provided in the course of a lawsuit. The following chapter outlines areas in which the trainer should make a concerted effort in documentation and recordkeeping.

EMPLOYEE FILES

Personal fitness trainers should make it a standard practice to keep detailed employee files. Thorough, complete and accurate employee files will be useful in the event that employee competency is challenged in a court of law. Each individual employee file should contain proof of a minimum level of competency reflected by such documents as the employment application, a current resume (within six months and kept current), proof of current CPR, first-aid and other certifications, membership in professional organizations, and documents reflecting an attainment of continuing education credits or the equivalent.

The employee file should also contain a signed and dated independent contractor/employee agreement that contains an adequate covenant not to compete/ pirate, *see* Chapter 4, *supra*. In the case of independent contractors, along with the independent contractor agreement, proof of liability insurance should be included in the file and updated to reflect current coverage. In some circumstances, the personal trainer for the facility should be included in a liability insurance certificate as an additional named insured, or perhaps the other way around.

Employee evaluations, commendations, awards and/or disciplinary actions should also be maintained in the employee file. Along with the creation of adequate employee files, a system of periodic and regular review and updating and purging of unnecessary information should also be implemented. The trainer should take note that before purging anything in the employee file, program counsel should be consulted to assess the impact of state statutes and other laws pertaining to the destruction of records and to applicable statutes of limitation which may dictate a particular practice as to how long records have to be maintained. Medical type information as to employees, including that related to employer sponsored fitness activities, should also be maintained but in a separate and secure storage system. The requirements of the Americans With Disabilities Act (ADA) and similar state laws dictate such requirements.

CLIENT FILES

As stated above, thorough, complete and accurate files as reflected by written documentation and recordkeeping can provide the requisite proof necessary in a court of law to show that the personal fitness trainer followed the appropriate standard of care. As a measure of protection, the professional should ensure that each and every client file contain the following written documents:

1. signed informed consent form for exercise testing and/or exercise prescription;
2. signed prospective release of liability form;
3. signed assumption of risk form;

4. signed client release of information form for physician communications;
5. current health/medical/fitness history chart;
6. signed client contract and/or policies and procedures statement;
7. results of exercise tests/physical exams/health screenings;
8. exercise prescriptions or programming information/recommendations;
9. physician approval/recommendations;
10. copies of correspondence between client physician and trainer;
11. copies of correspondence between client and trainer;
12. daily client activity/progress charts;
13. client questions/trainer answers to questions;
14. trainer observations and notations pertaining to client's mood, any physical ailments, unusual responses to exercise, adherence to proper form, technique, diet recommendations, and exercise prescriptions;
15. health screening questions or forms.

A master file containing the above documents should be maintained and stored in a safe place. A duplicate file containing the client's health history chart, workout chart, results of exercise tests/assessments, physician recommendations, and exercise prescriptions can be created to be used by the trainers for reference when actually working with the client. Like those files accumulated for employees, client files should be preserved and maintained for a period of time which is recommended by a professional's legal counsel so as to coincide with applicable statute of limitations within which lawsuits might be filed.

EQUIPMENT AND FACILITIES INSPECTION LOG

Chapter 7 alerted the professional to the necessity of conducting periodic and regular inspection, maintenance, service and repair of both the equipment and facilities utilized in the program. The importance of documenting such inspection/maintenance reports should not be understated. Many injuries to program participants occur due to negligently maintained equipment and premises, *see e.g.,* Herbert and Herbert, "Frequent Claims and Suits in Equipment-Related Injuries," *Fitness Management* at 22, February 1988; Herbert, "Legal Aspects of Fitness Premises Liability," *Fitness Management* at 18, September 1988. Such claims and suits are avoidable through a proper inspection and maintenance program.

Every program should maintain a daily/weekly equipment and facilities log in which any and all equipment/facility inspections, maintenance, service and repairs can be physically recorded. *See,* sample equipment and facilities logs in the Appendix. The logs should be dated, contain the name of the employee/person who conducted the inspection and/or performed the maintenance/repairs, list what equipment and facility areas were inspected and what maintenance or repairs were conducted. The inspector/repairman should be required to sign the log as well. For outside maintenance and repairs, a copy of the maintenance/repair order should be attached to the inspection log and the outside repairman should be required to sign and date the same. A daily and weekly inspection and maintenance schedule encompassing the above should be incorporated into program policies and procedures and be carried out in accordance therewith.

Although the sample equipment and facility logs contained in the Appendix are geared towards a typical fitness facility setting, they can be adapted to incorporate home/office training and outdoor training. As mentioned earlier in this chapter, the same principals and standards of care regarding inspection, maintenance and repair of equipment and facilities applies no matter what the setting. Usually for the home/office setting the equipment is minimal and can be inspected before every workout and within a matter of minutes. Since such equipment is not handling the volume of people that a typical club handles, weekly maintenance might replace daily maintenance. In fact, a client can be set up to do his/her own weekly maintenance log under some circumstances. Trainers should however, make sure to check such client log's regularly to ensure that the job was done. It should always be remembered to discontinue use of any broken or worn-out equipment until such equipment can be repaired or replaced.

EMPLOYEE POLICIES AND PROCEDURES MANUAL

The personal training program that utilizes employees should develop an employee policies and procedures manual by which the employment relationship and the delivery of service is governed. Such a manual should be drafted with the advice of program counsel, medical advisors and related fitness/health experts, and should be based upon applicable national standards, national employment laws, and state statutes/laws. Consideration must be given to a whole host of requirements including those dealing with the Family and Medical Leave Act, OSHA requirements and similar rights/responsibilities instituted by federal, state or local law. In general, the typical employee policies and procedures manual might cover the following areas:

1. thorough job classifications, delineations and descriptions should be outlined in the manual, including a system of employee hierarchy;

2. an outline of employee conduct on the job, including supervision/instruction procedures pertaining to the clientele;

3. an outline of procedures governing client pre-activity screening and fitness assessment;

4. a description of the informed consent, assumption of risk, and liability waiver process;

5. a general outline of the various exercise alternatives offered by the program;

6. a thorough outline of various procedures governing the different workout programs offered;

7. an outline of inspection/maintenance procedures to be followed regarding equipment and facilities;

8. an outline of emergency response protocols to be implemented in the event of an emergency/ accident;

9. an outline of employee qualification requirements regarding education, certification and continuing education;

10. a statement regarding a system of employee discipline/termination.

The foregoing is just a general sampling of some of the areas that can be addressed in an employee policies and procedures manual. Again, it must be stressed that program counsel should be consulted regarding the impact of national and state laws/statutes and precedents upon such a manual.

CLIENT POLICIES AND PROCEDURES STATEMENT

Every personal fitness trainer should expect his or her clients to adhere to certain program policies and procedures. To avoid confusion and misunderstandings concerning program policies and procedures, the trainer should develop a written client policies and procedures statement outlining the trainer's expectations of the client. The trainer should require that each new client sign and date the statement acknowledging receipt and agreement to the provisions.

An effective client policies and procedures statement might contain the following provisions:

1. an initial commitment to a number of training sessions;
2. the trainer's billing policy;
3. a provision outlining what forms must be completed before the program begins;
4. a twenty-four hour or similar cancellation policy;
5. a provision dealing with tardiness/no-shows;
6. the trainer's expectations of the client pertaining to number of workouts per week, training on off-days, reading educational articles, and nutritional aspects of the program;
7. a provision outlining the length of the workout session;
8. any charges over and above the rate per session, such as late payment fees, prorated travel time, and parking.

See also sample Client Policies and Procedures Statement contained in the Appendix.

FINAL THOUGHT

Thorough, complete and accurate documentation and recordkeeping implemented into the program will lend an air of professionalism to the program as well as help avoid confusion and misunderstandings with clients. Equally important is the fact that well documented records can be invaluable to the trainer in the event that competency is challenged in a court of law. When faced with the question of how much to document, the prudent trainer would be wise to err on the side of caution in being thorough with documentation and the procedures to be followed in the program. Unnecessary records can always be purged from the files at a later date based upon advice from program counsel.

Chapter 10

CONCLUSION

It is an exciting time to be in the personal fitness training business. The potential financial and professional rewards can far surpass what was traditionally available in the fitness industry. For the entrepreneurial minded trainer, the low start up costs involved in freelance private training, as well as the ability to turn a client's home or office into an exercise studio, allows one to open up his or her own fitness business without the need to finance an expansive exercise facility. An opportunity to train one private client typically leads to referrals and before long a full schedule of private sessions can be booked.

Unfortunately, many trainers who start to freelance find themselves ill equipped to handle the business and legal issues involved with any private enterprise. The trainer may start out training just one private client, and before he or she realizes it, has a burgeoning training business going. Due to the rapid development of such a clientele, the trainer typically finds him or herself training all day, leaving little time and energy to tend to the legal and business aspects involved in personal training. What usually develops is a strong clientele base but a weak legal/business base.

Personal fitness training is a business and must be treated as such if one is to have any measure of success.

It must also be well managed in order to avoid the legal and business pitfalls that plague even the most well-planned business undertakings. For the personal fitness trainer who is serious about making personal training a full-time career, that trainer must concentrate on working on his/her business as opposed to strictly working in it. Business plans should be carefully mapped out and constantly updated and revised. The legal structure of the business must be established. The business relationship with clients, employees and others must be spelled out, nurtured and legally protected. Taxes must be paid and insurance needs addressed along with a variety of professional and legal concerns.

This process is really not as complicated or expensive as it might be with other business ventures. Typically the personal trainer's clientele includes business professionals, lawyers, doctors and accountants who can be consulted. Perhaps a deal can be struck with some of these clients and services traded until the business is financially healthy. In any event, the need to address these issues is at the beginning before they get out of hand.

The personal trainer of the future will also be faced with some professional challenges as well. A more sophisticated and diverse fitness consumer is demanding highly qualified and experienced trainers to help them achieve their fitness and health goals. Not many people are willing to pay $50 and better an hour for a glorified "spotter," The trainer of the 1990s will need to be highly qualified, motivated and adaptable to meet the fitness needs of today's educated and aging baby-boomers. It is not enough in today's fitness market to be well versed in just weight training or aerobics. Today's aging population is demanding less stressful exercise such as walking, aquatic activity and stretching/flexibility routines. For more agile and youthful clients, cross-training may be important. For those clients, the trainer may need to have hands-on experience with cycling, swimming and running as well as strength and aerobic endurance exercises.

Education and certification appear to be the keys to establishing a minimum level of competency for fitness professionals in general. This may be particularly true for personal trainers. Due to the fact that a personal trainer could be held to a higher standard of care than a typical health club attendant, he or she should strive for the highest distinctions in the profession. Yet, certification and education is only a start. Continuing education and active involvement in national fitness organizations is necessary to stay on top of this ever changing and expanding field.

With all the recent talk about the need for education, certification and continuing education in the field, confusion still exists as to what exactly is the standard of care for fitness professionals, or for personal trainers to be specific. At this time there does not appear to be a universal and clearcut national standard of care for this subset of the fitness field nor for the whole field in general. In fact, competing standards of care presently exist, and at times conflict with one another. This causes confusion for the consumer shopping for the services of a trainer who may have to distinguish between the merits of one certification over the other. The trainer also has to weigh competing certifications, organizations and educational programs in attempting to gain a minimum level of competency, while the court system has to rely on potential conflicting expert testimony when a trainer's conduct comes into question.

Many inside and outside observers suggest that licensing of fitness professionals may be the answer to these concerns. While licensing would lend an air of credibility and professionalism to the industry in much the same way as national certifications, state licensing may also result in what may be perceived as overregulation and the loss of a certain degree of autonomy that the field now enjoys. Individual state licensing could also further contribute to the confusion as to what the standard of care is for fitness professionals (*e.g.* what may be the standard of care in California may not necessarily be the same standard in Pennsylvania.)

As the licensing and certification debate continues, the most prudent course of action for the personal fitness trainer to take might be to strive for the highest degree of competency and professionalism available in the field today. This would appear to be a combination of education, certification by a nationally recognized certifying body, and continuing education and involvement in the profession. Special client populations may require an even more diverse background and specialized knowledge from the trainer.

Along with acquiring and maintaining the highest level of competency in the profession, as well as establishing a strong business structure, the personal fitness trainer needs to tend to the legal fitness of the business as well. Trainers along with other fitness professionals, are being taken to court by their clients for professional incompetencies. To combat potential liabilities, risk management policies and strategies need to be implemented into the trainer's programs and activities. Program counsel and medical advisors need to be brought into the picture and consulted. Informed consents and liability waivers need to be drafted by program counsel and implemented into the program. Pre-activity screening and fitness assessment procedures need to be established that conform to industry standards. Equipment and facilities need to be inspected and maintained. The whole process involved in training needs to be thoroughly documented in the event that a trainer's conduct comes under scrutiny.

It is hoped that this manual will educate trainers on their legal responsibilities and potential liabilities, and prompt them to seek out the appropriate professionals for advice. Tending to the legal fitness of the business early on will allow the trainer to have the freedom to provide the highest degree of service without the fear of legal problems paralyzing his or her professional judgment.

LEGAL GLOSSARY

AGENCY: A concept in law creating a relationship of principal-agent, master-servant whereby the agent/servant carries out duties for the principal/master. Duties carried out within the scope of authority are attributed to the principal/master who will be responsible for the negligent performance of such duties by the agent/servant, referred to in law as Respondeat Superior.

ASSUMPTION OF RISK: Like contributory negligence, assumption of risk can in a proper case, be a total defense to a cause of action upon the basis of negligence. Proof of such a defense requires a showing that a person, with full knowledge and appreciation of all major risks, proceeded with the act and in so doing, assumed the risks associated with the act. Such concepts are now for the most part merged into concepts of comparative negligence.

CAUSE OF ACTION: Right to sue or institute litigation.

CONTRACT: Syn: Agreement
A legally effective and supportable document or understanding. Usually a promise or performance bargained for and given in exchange for a promise or performance, supported by adequate consideration (something of value).

CONTRIBUTORY NEGLIGENCE: Negligence of the injured party which wholly or partially caused or contributed to that person's injury, generally brought about by that person's failure to protect himself/herself. In many

States, a person's contributory negligence may preclude any recovery on a cause of action predicated upon negligence or malpractice. In other states, contributory negligence may only lessen the amount of damages recovered by such a person. In a growing number of jurisdictions such negligence will often be "compared" with the other party's negligence, and damages awarded only on a proportionate basis. Such a system of damage recovery is referred to as "comparative negligence."

IMMUNITY FROM SUIT RECOVERY: Freedom from damages as a result of suit. Granted sometimes to government, charities or special groups of persons. Broad immunity has been eroded, if not almost totally abrogated, by evolving interpretations of the Constitution, and federal and state statutes due to changing socio-economic and legal factors.

New immunity laws have been granted in many states, however, protecting so-called "good samaritans," volunteers and others who come to the emergency aid of injured parties, or who volunteer their time for others. These laws protect such persons from successful suit by the injured party in the event of injury, but only where the provider did not contribute to or cause the original injury.

INFORMED CONSENT: A voluntary agreement from a legally competent person (adult and mentally fit) who knows and fully understands all major risks associated with the consent to undergo a particular procedure. In law, determined subjectively, *i.e.,* did this particular person as opposed to a so-called ordinary reasonable man, know and understand, with full knowledge and appreciation of the facts, what risks were associated with the procedure.

LOSS OF CONSORTIUM: A cause of action of a husband or wife for injury to the marital relationship with his or her spouse due to the negligence of some party causing injury to that spouse. It is a separate cause of action, but is associated with the spouse's main cause of action.

In some states, a cause of action may be predicated upon a loss of consortium type claim brought by children of the injured party. In this situation, the cause of action amounts to interference with the parent/child relationship and the love and affection inherent in such situations.

MALPRACTICE: Negligence of a certain defined professional, *e.g.,* physicians, dentists, attorneys, architects, accountants (exercise specialists, personal fitness trainers ???).

NEGLIGENCE: Failure to conform one's conduct to a generally accepted standard or duty. Standard or duty may be established by law, *e.g.,* traffic laws (everyone must stop at red light), or by facts (specialty situations such as airplane crashes or "sponge left in body" situations where proof of facts automatically and presumptively establishes, simultaneously, duty & breach thereof), or by expert opinion, professional guidelines or standards.

NEGLIGENCE AS A CAUSE OF ACTION: One's failure to exercise due care to protect another person to whom the former owed a duty or responsibility where the failure proximately caused injury to the latter person.

RELEASE: A form of contract by which one person gives up certain rights or claims in exchange for a promise or performance, such as monetary payment. Generally, in medical or quasi-medical settings releases may not be effectively given prospectively or without adequate consideration. Usually, releases are given to settle claims or lawsuits based upon such claims.

THE PRACTICE OF MEDICINE: Diagnosis of an individual's symptoms to determine what disease or ailment he is afflicted with, and then to determine, upon the basis of that information, what remedy or treatment that should be given or prescribed to treat or correct his disease. Universally defined by law, *see, e.g.,* Ohio Revised Code Sec. 4731.34:

> "A person shall be regarded as practicing medicine...who examines or diagnoses for compensation of any kind, or prescribes, advises or recommends, administers or dispenses for compensation of any kind, direct or indirect, a drug or medicine, appliance mold or cast, application, operation or treatment, of whatever nature, for the care or relief of a wound, fracture or bodily injury, infirmity or disease..."

Note: Such statutes are very broadly written, all-encompassing, and are usually interpreted in like fashion by the courts.

TORT: An actionable wrong.

UNAUTHORIZED PRACTICE OF MEDICINE: The practice of medicine by an unlicensed individual. Generally a crime, usually a misdemeanor punishable by fine and/or incarceration in a penal institution for less than one year.

Sample
HYPOTHETICAL LIABILITY QUESTIONS
for Personal Fitness Trainers

HYPOTHETICAL LIABILITY QUESTIONS AND DISCUSSION FOR PERSONAL FITNESS TRAINERS

Q: What if I'm training a client in his home and he drops a weight on his foot - Am I liable?

Personal fitness trainers have a duty to provide supervision and instruction to clients. The supervision should include continuous attention in close proximity to the client. That does not mean instructing the client in weight training from across the room. Trainers should be providing continuous spotting, even for the most veteran of clients.

The instruction should adhere to the standards of "adequate" and "proper". "Adequate" refers to the amount of instruction and directions given before, during and after exercise. Was the client adequately instructed on correct form and handling of the weight, both during execution of the exercise and when returning the weight to the floor or rack?

"Proper" instruction pertains to the accuracy and correctness of the instruction and directions. Is the client being taught methods and qualifications in line with industry standards? Did the trainer use a weight that the client could reasonably handle or be expected to handle?

Even if the requisite amount of supervision and instruction is provided, a trainer still needs to protect himself/herself with the appropriate documentation. Adequate informed consent outlining the activity risks, as well as the proper use of prospective release and assumption of risk documents should be researched and drafted by local program counsel, where applicable.

Q: What happens if I take a client bike riding in the park and she gets injured - Am I liable?

First of all, a personal fitness trainer needs to be aware of the duty to ensure that the client has received adequate and proper instruction, as outlined above, as to any and all activities carried on during the course of the professional relationship. In this respect, the trainer needs to address certain issues – Has the client been adequately instructed on the rudiments of safe biking and the potential dangers involved in the sport of cycling?

Secondly, the trainer should make sure that the client's equipment is in good working order. The bike must be inspected and tested to make sure that it is in good working order and free from any harmful or dangerous condition. Trainers should insist that the client become familiar with the mechanics of the bike before activity. Also, the client needs to be equipped with the proper safety equipment such as a helmet, cycling shoes, gloves, protective glasses and so forth.

Lastly, the broad area of the law known as premises liability may apply to the above scenario. Trainers may have a duty to inspect the premises being used (the park) and either correct any dangerous condition or warn of those dangers that a reasonable inspection would disclose. Although there usually is no duty to warn of obvious dangers, it would be wise for the trainer to cover all bases and warn of both known and obvious dangers. Prior to the ride, trainers should thoroughly familiar with the course in question.

Trainers who encounter the above situation will need to prove that he or she followed the appropriate procedures in accordance with the standard of care. It would also be wise to have local legal counsel draft appropriate informed consents, prospective releases and other related program documents to provide proper protection to the trainer in the event of untoward incidents.

Q. I'm training a client in her home. Her child enters the room, trips over a piece of equipment, falls and is injured. Am I liable?

The above synopsis on premises liability could also be applied in this situation. Although a piece of equipment could be considered an obvious danger, it should be remembered that when a young child is involved, that child may not be cognizant of such dangers. Trainers may have a duty to warn a child entering an activity area of hazards or remove any obstacles, such as weights, that may be in the child's path that are likely to cause injury.

"But I'm training the client, not her daughter" trainers may bemoan, "just how far does my liability stretch?" Even though it is the client who is being trained and to whom the duty is principally owed, it is still foreseeable that the client's child could enter the room and be injured. If the injury occurs due to the trainer's negligence, trainers may very well be held liable for foreseeable injuries that occur within a so-called "zone of danger," that being the exercise room or area. It should also be remembered that since that area may be technically the trainer's – or under his or her control – that the trainer may well be liable for injuries which arise thereon, depending upon the status of the injured party (business invitee, guest, or trespasser).

The best way to safeguard against the above scenario is to have a strict policy that no unauthorized person enter the room during the workout. In the event that someone does enter the room, a thorough inspection of the exercise room and equipment beforehand should have revealed any hazards. Armed with this knowledge, a trainer can at least either correct such problems and dangers or warn against them. It is always better to error on the side of caution, and keep the workout area as free from as many obstacles as is practical and to keep unauthorized persons out of the area.

Q: *What's my liability if a client suffers a heart problem during a workout?*

In order to address this issue, let us assume that all of the current standards and protocols on screening, fitness, assessment and training techniques have been followed – yet the client suffers a heart problem. Let's further assume that there is nothing that a trainer could have done to avoid or prevent this from happening. Under these circumstances the trainer would not generally be held accountable. However, since this untoward event would occur in the privacy of the client's home, the trainer conducting the one-to-one session must be adequately prepared to deal with such emergencies personally.

Policies and procedures, including emergency response protocols, must be developed and implemented in advance to deal with the occurrence of accidents and emergencies during the rendition of services off-site. Such emergency response protocols should include current CPR and first aid training and certification for the trainer as well as knowledge of and immediate access to the closest emergency medical facilities and professionals. The responsible trainer should develop such comprehensive policies and procedures with the advice of both program counsel and various health professionals. If such policies and procedures are in place and properly formulated and carried out in the event of any danger, the trainer's liability should be minimal.

Q. I recommend that a client buy an exercise bike to work out alone at home. She buys the bike and is injured while riding it.

This specific question brings to light two areas of concern. First of all, by recommending equipment, the client is relying on your breadth of knowledge and "expertise" in the exercise equipment field. If a trainer has limited or no knowledge of the equipment being recommending and he or she makes a negligent recommendation (the equipment which the trainer suggested is dangerously defective) and the client is injured due to that negligent recommendation, the trainer could very well be held liable. If a trainer is going to branch out into exercise equipment consulting, he or she should become qualified on the equipment which is to be recommended. Equipment should be thoroughly tested prior to use and the trainer should become familiar with the literature and specifications as to equipment recommended or used. The trainer should also be in a position to document and substantiate why a specific piece of equipment was recommended over a competitor's brand. Trainers must keep up to date on industry tests and reports on exercise equipment.

Once equipment is recommended, trainers still have the duty to ensure that the client knows how to properly operate the equipment. The trainer must insist that the client undergo a series of instructional sessions with a trainer to learn the proper techniques in operating the bike or equipment in question. If all of these steps have been followed, the trainer's liability should be minimal. However, claims and litigation involving home exercise equipment remains a potential problem for all in this industry. There are simply no guarantees.

Q. Will my liability insurance policy cover the various sites that I might use for training clients?

Personal trainers are now able to get group rated professional liability insurance policies through such organizations as ACE and ACSM as well as others. Many of these policies provide million dollar liability coverage limits. Yet, just how far do these policies go in scope of coverage?

Trainers should be cautioned to use their professional judgment when taking a client out of a controlled environment to train. Although some policies appear to cover the trainer in the client's home and office, there are no similar clear-cut answers when one goes off-site to train a client. Not all off-site activities or environments will necessarily fall under the protection of a policy's coverage.

Trainers should stick within the normal confines of exercise, and should avoid teaching dangerous activities in dangerous environments, such as mountain climbing or ocean swimming. Trainers with specific questions about their liability policies should consult directly with their insurance carrier.

Q. I'm a personal trainer at a local health club looking to do some part-time freelance training. What steps should I take in setting up the business?

First of all, you should develop a basic business plan summary that outlines the trainer's mission statement, as well as his or her goals and objectives in going solo. Secondly, since this is a part-time venture, it might be advisable to initially set up shop as a sole proprietor. A sole proprietorship is the least complicated and expensive of the various business entities to set up and operate. However, if a trainer is to do business under an assumed or fictitious name, such a trade or fictitious name might have to be registered with appropriate state officials.

Trainers doing freelance work will also want to procure adequate insurance to cover freelance activities before taking on outside clients. Associations may be able to help with such coverage as well as private insurance brokers or agents.

Necessary documents, including informed consents, liability waivers, client policies and procedures, health history forms, and related program documents will also have to be prepared. These documents can be developed with advice of local program counsel. No business venture such as this should begin without consulting with a knowledgeable attorney and a CPA.

Q. If my clients sign a liability waiver, can they still sue me?

Anyone can sue anybody for anything at any time in this country. They may not always win, but the courts are open for such actions. A liability waiver does not give trainers blanket protection against a lawsuit. In the first place, courts have traditionally looked upon such waivers unfavorably, so there is a good chance that the waiver may not be upheld under any circumstance. Although it appears that the traditional view as to the use of such waivers is changing in favor of the use of such documents, even in those jurisdictions which have upheld waivers, such documents must contain very clear and concise language, and unambiguously and explicitly set forth the range of activities to which the release is to apply. That is why it is extremely important to have an experienced attorney draft the appropriate forms in accordance with state law. The chances are that trainers may not be able to absolve themselves totally from negligence by using a liability release form prepared by themselves without legal assistance and due regard for the particular nuances and requirements of local law.

Q: *My client asks me to put him on a "diet". Are there any liability problems associated with providing such advice?*

Possibly. Unless you are a registered dietician or other licensed professional, a trainer may want to refrain from putting a client on a specific diet or nutritional plan, especially for improvement of client health or to correct some adverse condition. The rendition of dieting advice can expose the trainer to an unauthorized practice of medicine or some other health care discipline claim. In some states it may be advisable to forego prescribing or recommending any type of diet for a client. Instead trainers may want to concentrate on educating the client on the fundamentals of good nutrition. Trainers may want clients to change their eating habits and patterns and to make lifelong nutritional changes rather than rely on the quick fix of diets. This approach will be "legally" safer in the long run for both the trainer and his/her client.

Q: *Will certification help me in the event that a client sues me for an injury?*

That depends. At the very least, certification as a personal trainer by a national certifying body may provide a minimum level of competence by which professional conduct may be judged in a court of law. At most, certification may become the national standard by which a trainer's conduct is scrutinized, but this has not occurred yet. In any event, certification will be used as one tool, along with degree status, continuing education, licensure where applicable, and experience to distinguish the qualified from the unqualified. But remember, if conduct falls below whatever the minimum level of competency is determined to be, trainers will more than likely be judged to be liable, whether certified or not.

Q: *Am I allowed to use the term "personal fitness trainer" if I am not certified as such?*

Since there are generally no laws regulating the practice of personal fitness training, no state licensure laws prohibit the use of the term; however, in at least one state, *i.e.,* Mississippi, the use of the term "trainer" is limited for use by those who are licensed in that state as athletic trainers. Consequently, in at least that state, other terms such as "personal fitness consultant" or "personal fitness professional" would have to be used by professionals.

Sample
CLIENT FORMS AND DOCUMENTS

Form Notation

No form or procedure should ever be adopted or initiated by a personal fitness trainer for personal fitness training activities without individualized legal and professional assistance. The law varies from state to state and develops over time. It is dependent upon matters of fact and judgment – As a consequence, legal and other professional advice is absolutely necessary for the development and use of any form or document. The following forms and documents are illustrative only.

Personal Fitness Trainer's Sample

PRE-WORKOUT INTERVIEW PROCEDURE FOR CLIENTS

1. Set up a mutually convenient pre-workout interview with the client to discuss our program and the client's goals, assess the client's health/fitness/medical history, and generally set the client at ease about exercise and begin to gain the client's confidence and trust. This is a critical first impression to establishing a long-term relationship with the client. Handle them with kid gloves, but be thorough, professional and personable! The initial interview should be in a relaxed, non-threatening environment (preferably the client's home as this is where they are most relaxed.)

2. During the interview, take notes on the client's goals, aspirations and anything else of value that might be of help in working with and motivating this person.

3. As the interview winds down, take the client's health/fitness/medical history on our preprinted form. Be sure to supplement the form with your own notes if a question or condition arises that is not noted on the form. Make sure to note any additional questions on the back of the form. Do not leave any question unanswered. Strongly recommend that the client undergo a physical examination and a graded exercise test by their physician before starting their program. Inform the client that we can recommend a physician who can perform a graded exercise stress test for them. Also inform the client that you may be doing initial tests on your own during the first meeting to test/assess their flexibility, strength and cardio-

vascular levels of fitness, as well as their percentage of body fat, present weight and measurements. If a question requires medical consultation (such as a patient's cholesterol count) stress that we require that such data be supplied to us as soon as possible, even if it requires a new test or a doctors' consultation. Also, make sure that the PAR-Q coronary risk factor analysis form is completed at this time. If the PAR-Q answers indicate a need for physician clearance, so advise the client, provide the Physician's Approval form and advise the client to contact you as soon as the clearance is secured. Upon recontact and submission of the form, complete this interview and the document execution process. Explain to the client that the medical approval portion of the document must be signed by their doctor before their first workout begins.

4. After the health/fitness medical history is taken, have the client read and sign the client policies and procedures form, answering any questions the client might have.
5. After the policies and procedures form is signed, have the client read and sign the informed consent form. Make sure you fully explain the risks involved as well as answer any questions that the client has and note the questions and answers where provided for on the form. Make sure the client fully understands what they are consenting to, even if you have to explain the whole document to them.
6. After the informed consent is read and signed, have the client read and sign the assumption of risk form for activity to be carried out during the course of the program. Again, make sure the client understands what they are signing and what risks they are assum-

ing. Make sure you fully explain the risks being assumed as well as answer any questions that the client has and note the questions and answers where provided for on the form.

7. After the assumption of risk form is read and signed, have the client read and sign the agreement and release of liability form. Make sure the client initials each and every paragraph. Again, make sure the client understands what he/she is signing and that he or she is releasing us in advance of activity from all right to sue and recover from various acts or omissions, including those arising from negligence.

8. If the client hasn't exhibited any coronary risk factors or other problems and conditions that would require further medical testing, screening and physical approval before we could or would take on that client, then set up the first workout. [Some programs may wish to have all clients secure physician clearance before proceeding.]

*** **THE FOLLOWING PROCEDURES MUST BE COMPLETED AND THE CLIENT MUST HAVE SIGNED ALL THE NECESSARY FORMS, INCLUDING THE MEDICAL APPROVAL FORM SIGNED BY THEIR DOCTOR, BEFORE THEY CAN BEGIN THEIR PROGRAM!**

NO EXCEPTIONS!!!

Personal Fitness Trainer's Sample

POLICIES AND PROCEDURES

1. Each new client must commit to an introductory package of 12 workouts. All introductory packages must be paid for in advance before the client can begin the program.

2. All forms including Health History Charts, Coronary Risk Analysis Forms, Informed Consents, Assumptions of Risk, Releases/Waivers and Medical Clearance Forms will be filled out in full and signed prior to the commencement of this program.

3. The program director will interview clients, take the health/medical history, and personally design workout programs. The program director may also initially start clients on programs. A trainer will then be specifically selected for the clients' personal goals and needs. If for any reason this trainer does not suit a client's needs, another will be provided. Clients will be asked to evaluate trainers on a form provided. Any trainer receiving two consecutive poor evaluations will be removed as trainer, and another will be provided.

4. No-shows or cancellations received less than twenty-four (24) hours before a scheduled workout will be charged to the client. If the trainer cancels with less than twenty-four (24) hours advance notice or fails to show for a scheduled workout, the rescheduled session will be at no charge to the client.

5. The client is expected to be punctual and understand that the trainer may have appointments immediately following their workout. As a courtesy to the next client, the client understands that tardiness will result

in the normal length of their workout being cut short. The client understands that the trainer is not obligated to stay past the allotted time scheduled for the workout. If both the client and the trainer have time for a full workout, the client will be charged an additional prorated amount for the time spent beyond the originally scheduled workout time. If the trainer is late, the length of the client's workout will not be affected. Habitual tardiness by the trainer will result in a free session to the client.

6. The client is expected to maintain a folder of all information and articles provided by the trainer for future reference.
7. The client is expected to maintain a daily diet log of everything the client eats or drinks, which will be checked by the trainer prior to every workout. The client is expected to be as specific and thorough as possible with regard to entries made in the diet log, including where the client ate/drank the item.
8. After the introductory program of 12 workouts is completed, the client will be billed for and must pay in advance for packages of 10 workouts at a time. The client will be billed towards the end of the current package of workouts, with payment due on receipt of invoice. The client will not be permitted to workout unless payment is received in advance.
9. Each workout session lasts 45 minutes unless a shorter or longer time has been agreed upon.

I HAVE READ THE ABOVE POLICIES AND PROCEDURES AND AGREE TO ABIDE BY THEM:

______________________________ Date: ____________
Client's Signature

Personal Fitness Trainer's Sample

HEALTH/MEDICAL HISTORY QUESTIONNAIRE

Name

Address

( ) - ( ) -
Phone (home) (work)

Age Birthdate Occupation

Physician's Name

Physician's Address Phone

Health/Fitness History

1. Are you presently involved in a regular exercise program?

   If yes, please list activity, duration, frequency and intensity:

2. Do you now or have you ever smoked? ____ YES ____ NO

   (a) If you previously smoked, how long did you smoke, how often, and when did you quit?

   (b) If you currently smoke, how much?

3. Do you use alcohol? ____ YES ____ NO

   (a) If yes, how much per day? _____
   How much per week? _____

4. Do you drink Caffeinated coffee or colas? ____ YES ____ NO

   (a) If yes, how much per day? _____

5. Are you now or have you ever been on a diet? ___YES ___NO

   (a) If yes, please explain

6. Do you consider yourself overweight or underweight? *(please circle)*

7. Number of meals you usually eat per day: _____

8. Do you usually eat breakfast? ____ YES ____ NO

9. Number of eggs you eat per week: _____

10. Number of times per week you usually eat the following:

    Beef: ____ Fish: ____ Pork: ____ Fowl: ____ Desserts: ____
    Fried Foods: ____ Fast Foods: ____

11. Do you regularly use any of the following: *(please circle)*

    butter sugar sweeteners salt whole milk

12. Do you consider yourself: *(please circle)*

    sedentary lightly active moderately active highly active

13. How would you describe your nutrition habits? *(please circle)*

    good fair poor

14. Would you characterize your life as: *(please circle)*

    highly stressful moderately stressful low in stress

15. Please describe your knowledge of exercise, and fitness: *(please circle)*

very knowledgeable knowledgeable no knowledge

16. Please describe your knowledge of nutrition: *(please circle)*

very knowledgeable knowledgeable no knowledge

Medical History

Present and Past History

1. Do you now have, have you recently experienced, or have you ever had:

(check in front of those questions to which you answer yes. Leave others blank)

_____ Heart attack, coronary bypass, or other cardiac surgery
_____ Diabetes
_____ Stroke
_____ Peripheral vascular disease
_____ Phlebitis, emboli
_____ Rheumatic fever
_____ High Blood Pressure
_____ Low Blood Pressure
_____ Chest discomfort
_____ Extra, skipped or rapid heart beats/palpitations
_____ Heart murmurs
_____ Ankle swelling
_____ Cold hands or feet
_____ Unusual shortness of breath
_____ Light-headedness or fainting
_____ Epilepsy, seizures
_____ Anemia
_____ Asthma
_____ Emphysema
_____ Bronchitis
_____ Pneumonia
_____ A chronic recurrent cough
_____ Increased anxiety or depression
_____ Emotional disorders

_____ Fatigue, lack of energy
_____ Trouble sleeping
_____ Migraine or recurrent headaches
_____ Swollen, stiff, or painful joints
_____ Foot problems
_____ Knee problems
_____ Back problems
_____ Shoulder problems
_____ Neck Problems
_____ Broken bones
_____ Ulcers
_____ Stomach or intestinal problems
_____ Hernia
_____ Limited range of motion in joints
_____ Arthritis
_____ Bursitis

IF YES TO ANY OF THE ABOVE, PLEASE EXPLAIN:

2. Please list any prescribed medications you are now taking:

3. Please list any over the counter medications or dietary supplements you are now taking:

4. Please list any illness, hospitalization or surgical procedure within the past two years:

5. Please list any drug allergies:

6. Please list date of last physical examination and results:

Family Medical History

1. Have any of your blood relatives had any of the following? (Please in front if yes) Include grandparents, parents, aunts, uncles and siblings:

_____ Heart attack
_____ Stroke
_____ Coronary disease
_____ Congenital heart disease
_____ High blood pressure
_____ Diabetes
_____ Coronary operations
_____ Elevated cholesterol

IF YES TO ANY OF THE ABOVE, PLEASE LIST RELATIVE AND AT WHAT AGE:

Fitness Goals

***Please describe specific goals and dates for achieving them.

_____ Improve strength
_____ Improve flexibility
_____ Improve cardiovascular fitness
_____ Improve muscle tone and shape
_____ Improve diet/eating habits
_____ Lose weight/inches
_____ Gain weight/muscle
_____ Reduce stress
_____ Increase energy
_____ Stop smoking/drinking
_____ Injury prevention

_____ Rehabilitate injury
_____ Additional goals (list): ______________________________

Nutritional Profile

Write down everything you eat or drink in the next 24 hour period. Indicate approximate amounts, how food was prepared (fried or baked), food quality (skim milk vs. whole milk, fresh vegetables vs. canned) and so forth. Be as specific as possible. Indicate where eaten as well.

BREAKFAST:

MID-MORNING:

LUNCH:

MID-AFTERNOON:

DINNER:

SNACK:

Personal Fitness Trainer's Sample

RISK FACTOR QUESTIONNAIRE

YES	NO	
____	____	1. Have you ever had, or has your doctor ever diagnosed you as having heart trouble or coronary disease?
____	____	2. Do you have a family history of heart problems or coronary disease?
____	____	3. Do you have a history of high blood pressure (above 145/90)?
____	____	4. Do you have diabetes?
____	____	5. Do you smoke cigarettes?
____	____	6. Are you overweight?
____	____	7. Is your diet heavy in fatty foods and red meat?
____	____	8. Do you ever have pains in your heart/chest?
____	____	9. Do you ever feel faint or have dizzy spells?
____	____	10. Has your doctor ever said you have high cholesterol?
____	____	11. Are you over 65 and sedentary?
____	____	12. Resting ECG: ________
____	____	13. Total cholesterol/HDL ratio: _______

Personal Fitness Trainer's Sample

PHYSICIAN'S APPROVAL FORM

_________________________________ has medical approval to participate in fitness programs and in the use of exercise equipment at various sites, including home or office, that may be provided by and/or recommended by _____________________.

The following restrictions apply (if none, so state):

____

Physician's Signature

____

Physician's Name

____

Street Address

____

City State Zip

Phone _______________

Date _______________

*** Please attach a copy of the results of the latest physical examination

Personal Fitness Trainer's Sample

RELEASE OF INFORMATION FORM

To Whom It May Concern:

Please be advised that ____________________ and any member, associate or designee of that firm are hereby authorized to inspect and copy or be furnished copies of any and all hospital, dental or medical records of any sort, charts, notes, medical bills, dental bills, x-rays, lab reports and prescriptions and are to be furnished any and all other information without limitation pertaining to any confinement, examination, treatment or condition of myself, including medical, dental, psychological or other treatment, examinations, or counseling for any condition, medical, dental or psychological.

This AUTHORIZATION shall be considered as continuing and you may rely on it in all respects unless you have previously been advised by me in writing to the contrary. It is expressly understood by the undersigned and you are hereby authorized to accept a copy or photocopy of this medical authorization with the same validity as though an original had been presented to you.

Dated this _____ day of __________, 19___.

X________________________

Personal Fitness Trainer's Sample

INFORMED CONSENT FOR PARTICIPATION IN A PERSONAL FITNESS TRAINING PROGRAM FOR APPARENTLY HEALTHY ADULTS

(without known or suspected heart disease)

Name____

1. Purpose and Explanation of Procedure

I hereby consent to voluntarily engage in an acceptable plan of personal fitness training. I also give consent to be placed in personal fitness training program activities which are recommended to me for improvement of my general health and well-being. These may include dietary counseling, stress management, and health/fitness education activities. The levels of exercise I perform will be based upon my cardiorespiratory (heart and lungs) and muscular fitness. I understand that I may be required to undergo a graded exercise test as well as other fitness tests prior to the start of my personal fitness training program in order to evaluate and assess my present level of fitness. I will be given exact personal instructions regarding the amount and kind of exercise I should do. I agree to participate three times per week in the formal program sessions. Professionally trained personal fitness trainers will provide leadership to direct my activities, monitor my performance, and otherwise evaluate my effort. Depending upon my health status, I may or may not be required to have my blood pressure and heart rate evaluated during these sessions to regulate my exercise within desired limits. I understand that

I am expected to attend every session and to follow staff instructions with regard to exercise, diet, stress management, and other health and fitness related programs. If I am taking prescribed medications, I have already so informed the program staff and further agree to so inform them promptly of any changes which my doctor or I have made with regard to use of these. I will be given the opportunity for periodic assessment and evaluation at regular intervals after the start of my program.

I have been informed that during my participation in the above described personal fitness training program, I will be asked to complete the physical activities unless symptoms such as fatigue, shortness of breath, chest discomfort or similar occurrences appear. At that point, I have been advised that it is my complete right to decrease or stop exercise and that it is my obligation to inform the personal fitness training program personnel of my symptoms. I hereby state that I have been so advised and agree to inform the personal fitness training program personnel of my symptoms, should any develop.

I understand that during the performance of exercise, a personal fitness trainer will periodically monitor my performance and, perhaps measure my pulse, blood pressure or assess my feelings of effort for the purposes of monitoring my progress. I also understand that the personal fitness trainer may reduce or stop my exercise program, when any of these findings so indicate that this should be done for my safety and benefit.

I also understand that during the performance of my personal fitness training program, physical touching and positioning of my body may be necessary to assess my muscular and bodily reactions to specific exercises, as well as ensure that I am using proper technique and body alignment. I expressly consent to the physical contact for the stated reasons above.

2. **Risks**

It is my understanding and I have been informed that there exists the remote possibility during exercise of adverse changes including, but not limited to, abnormal blood pressure, fainting, dizziness, disorders of heart rhythm, and very rare instances of heart attack, stroke or even death. I further understand and I have been informed that there exists the risk of bodily injury including, but not limited to, injuries to the muscles, ligaments, tendons and joints of the body. Every effort I have been told, will be made to minimize these occurrences by proper staff assessments of my condition before each exercise session, staff supervision during exercise and by my own careful control of exercise efforts. I fully understand the risks associated with exercise, including the risk of bodily injury, heart attack, stroke or even death, but knowing these risks, it is my desire to participate as herein indicated.

3. **Benefits to be Expected and Alternative Available to Exercise**

I understand that this program may or may not benefit my physical fitness or general health. I recognize that involvement in the exercise sessions will allow me that involvement in the personal fitness training sessions will allow me to learn proper ways to perform conditioning exercises, use fitness equipment and regulate physical effort. These experiences should benefit me by indicating how my physical limitations may affect my ability to perform various physical activities. I further understand that if I closely follow the programs instructions, that I will likely improve my exercise capacity and fitness level after a period of 3 to 6 months.

4. **Confidentiality and Use of Information**

I have been informed that the information which is obtained in this personal fitness training program will be treated as privileged and confidential and will consequently not be released or revealed to any person without my express written consent. I do however agree to the use of any information which is not personally identifiable with me for research and statistical purposes so long as same does not identify my person or provide facts which could lead to my identification. I also agree to the use of any information for the purpose of consultation with other health and fitness professionals, including my doctor. Any other information obtained however, will be used by the program staff in the course of prescribing exercise for me and evaluating my progress in the program.

5. **Inquiries and Freedom of Consent**

I have been given an opportunity to ask certain questions as to the procedures of this program. Generally, these requests have been noted by the interviewing staff with his/her responses as follows:

____

____

____

I further understand that there are also other remote risks that may be associated with this personal fitness training program. Despite the fact that a complete accounting of all these remote risks have not been provided to me, it is still my desire to participate.

I acknowledge that I have read this document in its entirety or that it has been read to me if I have been unable to read same.

I expressly consent to the rendition of all services and procedures as explained herein by all program personnel.

Date: ____________________

____
Client's Signature

____

By ____________________
Its Authorized Representative

Personal Fitness Trainer's Sample

EXPRESS ASSUMPTION OF RISK FOR MY PARTICIPATION IN A PERSONAL FITNESS TRAINING PROGRAM

I, the undersigned, hereby expressly and affirmatively state that I wish to participate in the personal fitness training program of ____________. I realize that my participation in this activity involves risk of injury, including but not limited to bodily injuries, heart attack, stroke and even death. I also recognize that there are many other risks of injury including serious disabling injuries which may arise due to my participation in this activity and that it is not possible to specifically list each and every individual injury risk. However, knowing, understanding and appreciating the material risks and reasonably anticipating that other injuries and even death are a possibility, I hereby expressly assume all delineated risks of injury, all other possible risks of injury and even death which could occur by reason of my participation in this personal fitness training program.

I have also had an opportunity to ask questions. Any questions which I have asked have been answered to my complete satisfaction.

Date: _____________, 19___.

____
Participant

____

By: _________________________
Its Authorized Representative

NOTES OF QUESTIONS AND ANSWERS

____

____

____

____

This is as stated a true and accurate record of what was asked and answered.

____
Participant

TO BE CHECK BY PROGRAM STAFF

	CHECKED	INITIALED
I. Risks were orally discussed.	______	______
II. Questions were asked and the participant indicated complete understanding of the risks.	______	______
III. Questions were not asked, but an opportunity for questions was provided and the participant indicated complete understanding of the risks	______	______

Dated:__________, 19___ ____________________
Staff Member

Personal Fitness Trainer's Sample

AGREEMENT AND RELEASE OF LIABILITY

1. In consideration of being allowed to participate in the personal fitness training activities and programs of ______________________ and to use its facilities, equipment and services, in addition to the payment of any fee or charge, I do hereby forever waive, release and discharge ______________ and its officers, agents, employees, representatives, executors, and all others acting on their behalf from any and all claims or liabilities for injuries or damages to my person and/or property, including those caused by the ordinary negligent act or omission of any of those mentioned or others acting on their behalf, arising out of or connected with my participation in any activities, programs or services of ________________, or the use of any equipment at various sites, including home, provided by and/or recommended by ______________. I understand that the terms of this release shall not apply to gross negligence, willful or wanton conduct or criminal activity. (PLEASE INITIAL___).

2. I have been informed of, understand and am aware that strength, flexibility and aerobic exercise, including the use of equipment, is a potentially hazardous activity. I also have been informed of, understand and am aware that fitness activities involve a risk of injury, including a remote risk of stroke, heart attack, death or serious disability, and that I am voluntarily participating in these activities and using equipment and machinery with full knowledge, understanding and appreciation of the dangers involved. I hereby

agree to expressly assume and accept any and all risks of injury or death. (PLEASE INITIAL ___).

3. I do hereby further declare myself to be physically sound and suffering from no condition, impairment, disease, infirmity or other illness that would prevent my participation or use of equipment or machinery. I do hereby acknowledge that I have been informed of the need for a physician's approval for my participation in the exercise activities, programs and use of exercise equipment. I also acknowledge that it has been recommended that I have a yearly or more frequent physical examination and consultation with my physician as to physical activity, exercise and use of exercise equipment. I acknowledge that I have either had a physical examination and have been given my physician's permission to participate, or that I have decided to participate in the exercise activities, programs and use of equipment without the approval of my physician and do hereby assume all responsibility for my participation in said activities, programs and use of equipment. (PLEASE INITIAL___).

4. I understand that __________ provision and maintenance of an exercise/fitness program for me does not constitute an acknowledgment, representation or indication of my physiological well-being, or a medical opinion relating thereto. (PLEASE INITIAL___).

5. In the event that any provisions of this agreement should be deemed to be invalid, then and in that event, the remaining terms hereof shall continue to be valid and enforceable between the parties hereto. (PLEASE INITIAL ___).

Agreed to this _____ day of _____________, 19___.

____
Client's Signature

____

By_____________________
Its Authorized Representative

Sample
BUSINESS FORMS
for Personal Fitness Trainers

Personal Fitness Trainer's Sample

EMPLOYMENT AGREEMENT

This Agreement ("Agreement") is made this ______ day of ____________________, 19__/20__ between ______________________________ ("Employer") and ______________________________ ("Employee").

RECITALS

The purpose of this Agreement is to state the terms and conditions under which the Employer/Employee relationship is created herein and to protect Employer's time and energy expended over the past years in developing its personal fitness training/consulting business, programs and clientele.

The fitness programs, business forms, subscribing client list, and any other related documents are considered trade secrets developed by Employer.

Employer is in the business of providing personal fitness training services, exercise and nutritional counseling, and sales of fitness equipment, products, and services.

Employer desires to have the above services performed by an Employee.

Employee agrees to perform those services for Employer under the terms and conditions set forth in this agreement.

Employer agrees to provide Employee with valuable training, experience, and knowledge in order to perform Employee's services hereunder.

THEREFORE, in consideration of the mutual promises and covenants set forth herein, Employer and Employee agree as follows:

1. **NATURE OF WORK**

Employee shall be employed as a PERSONAL FITNESS TRAINER, Employee shall perform services including, but not limited to, the following:

a. Instructing Employer's clients in safe, effective and proper exercise programs;

b. Training Employer's staff in safe, effective and proper exercise programs;

c. Promoting Employer's products and services at all times while in the employment of the Employer; and

d. Furthering and promoting Employer's business, fitness philosophy and policies and procedures.

2. **COMPENSATION**

Employer shall pay as compensation to Employee for services rendered hereunder, $__________ per client consultation session. In addition, Employer shall pay to Employee _____ percent (_____%) of the fee for any of Employer's products sold or additional services provided.

3. **OTHER BENEFITS**

Employer shall provide Employee with other benefits as outlined in Exhibit "A" attached hereto and incorporated herein by reference.

4. **EXPENSES**

Employer will further reimburse Employee for all reasonable expenses documented sufficiently for purposes of allowing Employer to deduct said expenses pursuant to the Internal Revenue Code as may be amended from time to time, and properly incurred by Employee after the date hereof and in the performance of Employee's duties hereunder.

5. **WITHHOLDING**

Employer shall be entitled to withhold amounts from any compensation, or other form of remuneration or benefit payable by Employer to Employee which Employer reasonably believes it is required to withhold under any federal, state, local or foreign tax law to which Employer may be subject.

6. **TIME AND EFFORTS**

Employee shall devote his/her productive time, energies and abilities to the proper and efficient performance of his/her duties. Without the prior express written authorization of Employer, Employee shall not, directly or indirectly, during the term of this Agreement:

a. Render services to any other person or firm, whether for compensation or otherwise, or;

b. Engage in any activity competitive with or adverse to Employer's business, whether alone, as a partner, or as an officer, director or employee of any other corporation.

7. **SOLICITING CLIENTS AFTER TERMINATION OF EMPLOYMENT**

Upon termination of this Agreement, Employee shall immediately cease training and consulting with any and all of Employer's clients. Employee shall not for a period of two (2) years immediately following the termination of employment with Employer, either directly or indirectly:

a. make known to any person, firm, or corporation the names and addresses of any of the clients of Employer or any other information pertaining to them; and/or

b. call on, solicit or take away, or attempt to call on, solicit, or take away any client of the Employer, past, present or future whom Employee knows of or has become acquainted with during Employee's employment with Employer, either for Employee or for any other person or corporation; and/or

c. call on, solicit or take away, or attempt to call on, solicit, or take away potential clients of the Employer.

8. **COMPETING WITH EMPLOYER**

Employee shall not for a period of two (2) years immediately following the termination of employment with Employer attempt in any manner either directly or indirectly to compete, or attempt to compete with Employer in personal fitness training activities in Employer's territories in the state of __________.

9. **RETURN OF EMPLOYER'S PROPERTY**

On the termination of Employee's employment or whenever requested by Employer, Employee shall immediately deliver to Employer all property in Employee's possession or control belonging to Employer.

10. **OWNERSHIP OF RECORDS, FORMS AND DOCUMENTS**

Any and all records, books, forms, accounts, programs and other documents relating in any manner whatsoever to the clients (past, present, future or potential) and/or business of Employer, whether purchased, prepared or developed by Employee or otherwise coming into Employee's possession, shall be the sole and exclusive property of Employer regardless of who actually prepared, developed or purchased the records, books, forms, accounts, programs or other documents. All such documents shall be immediately returned to Employer by Employee on any termination of Employee's employment or whenever requested by Employer.

11. **REFERRALS**

Employee understands that any referrals from clients of Employer are the sole property and business of the Employer. Employee shall not solicit for himself or herself, or on the behalf of any other person, corporation, partnership or business, referrals from Employer's clients during employment with Employer, and for a period of two (2) years immediately following termination of employment with the Employer.

12. **RECRUITING EMPLOYEES AFTER TERMINATION OF EMPLOYMENT**

Employee shall not for a period of two (2) years immediately following the termination of employment with Employer attempt in any manner either directly or indirectly to recruit, or attempt to recruit, any of the officers or employees, present or future, of Employer.

13. **DURATION**

This Agreement shall commence upon the date first written above and terminate upon the happening of any of the following events:

a. Upon the death or permanent disability of Employee.

b. Whenever Employer and Employee shall mutually agree to termination.

c. Upon thirty (30) days prior written notice by either Employer or Employee to the other, with or without cause.

d. Immediately upon written notice by Employer to Employee.

14. **REMEDIES**

Employee agrees that in the event of breach of any provisions of this Agreement, Employee shall be liable to Employer for any and all expenses, costs and reasonable attorneys' fees incurred to enforce Employer's rights under this Agreement plus the amount of loss, both direct and consequential, to Employer arising from or related to such breach.

15. **SEVERABILITY**

In the event that any one or more of the provisions contained in this Agreement shall for any reason be held to be invalid, illegal or unenforceable in any respect, such invalidity, illegality or unenforceability shall not affect any other provision thereof and this Agreement shall be construed as if such invalid, illegal, or unenforceable provision had never been contained herein.

16. **GOVERNING LAW**

This Agreement shall be construed in accordance with and governed by the laws of the State of ______________.

17. **AMENDMENTS**

This Agreement may not be modified or amended or any term or provision thereof waived or discharged except in writing and signed by both Employer and Employee.

18. **ENTIRE AGREEMENT**

This Agreement embodies the entire agreement between Employer and Employee and supersedes all prior written and/or oral agreements and understandings between Employer and Employee.

19. **ADDITIONAL PROVISIONS**

Employee shall maintain the following:

a. Current membership in, and certification by:

____

b. Current CPR certification.

IN WITNESS WHEREOF, the parties hereto have executed this Agreement as of the date above first written.

____
Name of Company

by: ______________________________
its Authorized Representative
"EMPLOYER"

____
"EMPLOYEE"

Personal Fitness Trainer's Sample

INDEPENDENT CONTRACTOR AGREEMENT

This Agreement ("Agreement") is made this ______ day of ____________________, 19__/20__ between ______________________________ ("Employer") and ______________________ ("Independent Contractor").

RECITALS

The purpose of this Agreement is to state the terms and conditions under which the Employer/Independent Contractor relationship is created herein and to protect Employer's time and energy expended over the past years in developing its personal fitness training/consulting business, programs and clientele.

The fitness programs, business forms, subscribing client list, and any other related documents are considered trade secrets developed by Employer.

Employer is in the business of providing personal fitness training services, exercise and nutritional counseling, and sales of fitness equipment, products, and services.

Employer desires to have the above services performed by an Independent Contractor.

Independent Contractor agrees to perform those services for Employer under the terms and conditions set forth in this agreement.

Employer agrees to provide Employee with valuable training, experience, and knowledge in order to perform Employee's services hereunder.

THEREFORE, in consideration of the mutual promises and covenants set forth herein, Employer and Employee agree as follows:

1. **NATURE OF WORK**

Independent Contractor shall be employed as a PERSONAL FITNESS TRAINER, Contractor shall perform services including, but not limited to, the following:

a. Instructing Employer's clients in safe, effective and proper exercise programs;

b. Providing safe, effective and proper nutritional counseling to Employer's clients;

c. Promoting Employer's products and services at all times while in the employment of the Employer; and,

d. Furthering and promoting Employer's business, fitness philosophy and policies and procedures.

2. **COMPENSATION**

As a PERSONAL FITNESS TRAINER, Employer shall pay as compensation to Independent Contractor for services rendered hereunder, $___________ per client consultation session. In addition, Employer shall pay to Independent Contractor, _______ percent (___%) of the fee for any of Employer's products sold or additional services provided.

3. **STATUS OF INDEPENDENT CONTRACTOR**

The parties intend that an Employer/Independent Contractor relationship be created by this Agreement. Employer is only interested in the results to be achieved, and the conduct and control of the work will lie solely with the Independent Contractor. Independent Contractor is not to be considered an agent or employee of Employer for any purpose. It is understood that Employer does not agree to use Independent Contractor exclusively. It is further understood that Independent Contractor is free to engage in the performance of his own personal client consultation pursuant to the terms and conditions of this Agreement. Independent Contractor agrees and covenants that in the performance of training, counseling, or advising personal clients, Independent Contractor shall not:

a. Train any personal client simultaneously with any of Employer's clients;

b. Wear Employer's uniform while training a personal client;

c. Use any of Employer's forms, charts, business cards, stationary, or any other related documents pertaining to Employer's business;

d. Represent to a personal client or act in any manner that tends to represent to the personal client that the client is being trained under the guidelines, principles, or formulas of Employer;

e. Engage in the unauthorized sale of any services, goods, or products on behalf of Employer. Independent Contractor agrees not to sell, offer to sell, or distribute, with or without compensation, any services, goods, or products of Employer except with the express approval of Employer.

4. **SOLICITING CLIENTS AFTER TERMINATION OF EMPLOYMENT**

Upon termination of this Agreement, Independent Contractor shall immediately cease training any and all of Employer's clients. Independent Contractor shall not for a period of one (1) year immediately following the termination of employment with Employer, either directly or indirectly:

a. make known to any person, firm, or corporation the names and addresses of any of the clients of the Employer or any other information pertaining to them; and/or

b. call on, solicit or take away, or attempt to call on, solicit, or take away any client of the Employer, past, present or future whom the Independent Contractor knows of or has become acquainted with during the Independent Contractor's employment with the Employer, either for the Independent Contractor or for any other person or corporation; and/or

c. call on, solicit or take away, or attempt to call on, solicit, or take away potential clients of the Employer.

5. **COMPETING WITH EMPLOYER**

Independent Contractor shall not both during Employment with Employer and for a period of one (1) year immediately following the termination of employment with Employer, attempt to compete with Employer in the personal fitness/consultation business in Employer's territories.

6. **RETURN OF EMPLOYER'S PROPERTY**

On the termination of Independent Contractor's employment or whenever requested by Employer, Independent Contractor shall immediately deliver to Employer all property in Independent Contractor's possession or control belonging to Employer.

7. **OWNERSHIP OF RECORDS, FORMS AND DOCUMENTS**

Any and all records, books, forms, accounts, programs and other documents relating in any manner whatsoever to the clients (past, present, future or potential) and/or business of Employer, whether purchased, prepared or developed by Independent Contractor or otherwise coming into Independent Contractor's possession, shall be the sole and exclusive property of Employer regardless of who actually prepared, developed or purchased the records, books, forms, accounts, programs or other documents. All such documents shall be immediately returned to Employer by Independent Contractor on any termination of Independent Contractor's employment or whenever requested by Employer. If Independent Contractor purchases any such original books or documents, he/she shall immediately notify Employer, who then shall immediately reimburse him/her.

8. **REFERRALS**

Independent Contractor understands that any referrals from clients of Employer are the sole property and business of the Employer. Independent Contractor shall not solicit for himself or herself, or on the behalf of any other person, corporation, partnership or business, referrals from Employer's clients during employment with Employer, and for a period of one (1) year immediately following termination of employment with Employer.

9. **RECRUITING EMPLOYEE'S AFTER TERMINATION OF EMPLOYMENT**

Independent Contractor shall not for a period of one (1) year immediately following the termination of employment with Employer attempt in any manner either directly or indirectly to recruit, or attempt to recruit, any of the officers or employees, present or future, of Employer.

10. **LIABILITY AND INDEMNIFICATION**

The work to be performed under this Agreement will be performed entirely at Independent Contractor's risk and independent Contractor agrees to provide his own professional liability insurance. Independent Contractor agrees to indemnify Employer for any and all liability or loss arising in any way out of the performance of the services of Independent Contractor under this Agreement.

11. LIABILITY FOR TAXES

Independent Contractor agrees that all state and federal withholding taxes, social security taxes, unemployment insurance contributions and assessments, worker's compensation insurance, general excise and sales taxes, self-employment taxes, and any and all other taxes, fees, assessments or contributions covering Independent Contractor, if any, shall be the sole responsibility of Independent Contractor.

12. DURATION

Either party may cancel this Agreement upon fifteen (15) days notice to the other.

13. MINIMUM COMMITMENT

Independent Contractor agrees to make himself or herself available to Employer to train a minimum of five (5) clients per week. Employer is not obligated to provide Independent Contractor with the minimum commitment stated above, but will make a good faith attempt to provide Independent Contractor with as many clients as Independent Contractor desires.

14. REMEDIES

Independent Contractor agrees that in the event of breach of any provision of this Agreement, Independent Contractor shall be liable to Employer for any and all expenses, costs and reasonable attorneys' fees incurred to enforce Employer's rights under this Agreement plus the amount of loss, both direct and consequential, to Employer arising from or related to such breach.

15. **SEVERABILITY**

In the event that any one or more of the provisions contained in this Agreement shall for any reason be held to be invalid, illegal, or unenforceable in any respect, such invalidity, illegality, or unenforceability shall not affect any other provision thereof and this Agreement shall be construed as if such invalid, illegal, or unenforceable provision had never been contained herein.

16. **ADDITIONAL PROVISIONS**

Independent Contractor shall maintain the following:

a. Current membership in, and certification by:

b. Current CPR certification;

c. His/her own professional liability insurance and health insurance;

IN WITNESS WHEREOF, the parties hereto have executed this Agreement as of the date above first written.

____

By______________________________
Its Authorized Representative
"EMPLOYER"

____
"INDEPENDENT CONTRACTOR"

Sample
RISK MANAGEMENT UTILIZATION FORMS
For Personal Fitness Trainers

Personal Fitness Trainer's Sample

EQUIPMENT LOG

Date: ____________________________

Employee: ____

Weight Equipment	**Inspected Maintenance/Repair**
1. Leg Extension	
2. Leg Curl	
3. Leg Press	
4. Chest Press	
5. Shoulder Press	
6. Lat Pulldown	
7. Arm Curl	
8. Tricep Extension	
9. Squat Racks	
10. Benches	
Aerobic Equipment	
1. Cycles	
2. Stair Climbers	
3. Rowers	

Employee's Signature: ____

Personal Fitness Trainer's Sample

FACILITY LOG

Date: ______________________

Employee: ____

Inspected Maintenance/Repair

1. **Weight Room Area:**
   Floors
   Signs
   Mirrors
   Other

2. **Aerobic Room Area:**
   Floors
   Signs
   Mirrors
   Other

3. **Locker Rooms:**
   Floors
   Shower Area
   Sinks, Mirrors
   Lockers
   Other

4. **Pool Area:**
   Pool
   Whirlpool
   Sauna
   Floors/Wet Areas
   Signs
   Other

5. **Entrance/Exit:**
   Entranceway
   Exits
   Signs
   Doors
   Reception Area
   Lounge Area

Employee's Signature: ________________________________

Personal Fitness Trainer's Sample

EXERCISE INSTRUCTIONS

BEGINNER'S WEIGHT TRAINING PROGRAM

WARM-UP:

1. Stationery Cycling - Used to warm-up legs, increase blood flow and slowly raise blood pressure to prepare for exercise.

- Adjust the seat so the client's leg is almost fully extended at the bottom of the pedal revolution. The knee should be slightly bent in this position.
- Client should lightly grasp cycle handles.
- Resistance level should be set at light to moderate.
- Have the client warm-up for five minutes, monitoring the client's heart rate and perceived exertion. Client should maintain HR of approximately 60-70% of max HR.

2. Static Stretching - Used to stretch and warm up muscles, tendons and ligaments.

- Run a client through safe, static stretching (no bouncing) of all major muscle groups for five minutes. Hold each stretch for 15-25 seconds.

LEGS:

1. Squats With No Weight - Used to work all major muscle groups of the legs.

- Stand feet shoulder width apart, feet slightly pointed outward.
- Hands on hips, head up, eyes forward, back straight all throughout the motion.
- Squat down until thighs are parallel with the floor (breathing in), returning to standing position (breathing out).
- Repeat for 1-2 sets of 15-25 repetitions.

2. Leg Extensions - Used to work the quadriceps

- Sit on leg extension machine, knees should be in line with axis of the machine, back flat against pad, feet pointed straight ahead.

UPPER BODY:

1. Dumbbell Chest Press – Primarily works the chest muscles (pectoralis major).

- Lie flat on bench, feet on ground, back flat and dumbbells to the side and straight across the chest, palms facing towards feet.
- Press dumbbells above chest while exhaling, extending arms straight out and bringing dumbbells together. Slowly lower to starting position while inhaling.
- Repeat for 1-2 sets of 8-12 repetitions.

2. Lat Pulldown – Primarily works muscles of upper back (latissimus dorsi).

- Take wide grip on bar and sit in seat.
- Fully extend arms above head, stretching upper back muscles.
- Exhale while bringing arms down and bar behind neck to top of shoulders.
- Slowly raise arms and bar above head to straight position while inhaling, again stretching upper back.
- Repeat for 1-2 sets of 8-12 repetitions.

3. Dumbbell Shoulder Press - Primarily works shoulder muscles (deltoids).

- Sit upright on bench, back straight and feet flat on floor.
- Raise dumbbells to shoulder height and straight across shoulders.
- Press dumbbells above head while exhaling until arms are fully extended, bringing dumbbells together.

- Slowly lower weights to shoulder height while inhaling.
- Repeat for 1-2 sets of 8-12 repetitions.
- Slowly lower weights to shoulder height while inhaling.
- Repeat for 1-2 sets of 8-12 repetitions.

4. Alternate Dumbbell Curls - Primarily works the biceps.

- Sit upright on bench, back straight and feet flat on floor, with knees and feet almost touching.
- Begin with dumbbells to the sides, palms facing in.
- Start with right side and curl weight up while exhaling, keeping elbow against the side of the body and slowly rotating palm up and slightly out.
- Slowly lower dumbbell to side while inhaling.
- Repeat for left side.
- Repeat for 1-2 sets of 8-12 repetitions for both arms.

5. Tricep Pressdowns - Primarily works tricep muscles.

- Stand upright, feet close together, back straight, grasp bar with a close grip and bring bar in close to the body to sternum.
- From sternum, press bar down while exhaling, keeping bar close to the body and fully extending the arms while contracting the triceps.
- Slowly raise bar back to sternum height while exhaling.
- Repeat for 1-2 sets of 8-12 repetitions.

COOLDOWN:

1. Stationery Cycling (see warm-up above) - Used to gradually bring HR down while preventing blood pooling and lactic acid build-up

- Have client cycle at a slow, easy pace for 5-10 minutes.

2. Static Stretching (see warm-up above) - Used to loosen tight fatigues muscles to prevent muscles cramping and lactic acid build-up.

- Run the client through safe, static stretching of all major muscle groups for five minutes.

SELECTED REFERENCES

Books

AFAA, **FIRST AID FOR THE FITNESS PROFESSIONAL** (AFAA Sherman Oaks, CA 1995).

American College of Sports Medicine, **GUIDELINES FOR GRADED EXERCISE TESTING AND EXERCISE PRESCRIPTION**, (Lea and Febiger, Philadelphia, PA, 5th Ed. 1995).

American College of Sports Medicine, **RESOURCE MANUAL FOR GUIDELINES FOR EXERCISE TESTING AND PRESCRIPTION**, Lea and Febiger, Philadelphia, PA, 3rd Ed. 1997).

American Heart Association, The Committee on Exercise, **EXERCISE TESTING AND TRAINING OF APPARENTLY HEALTHY INDIVIDUALS: A HANDBOOK FOR PHYSICIANS**, (Dallas, 1972).

American Heart Association, The Committee of Exercise, **EXERCISE TESTING AND TRAINING OF INDIVIDUALS WITH HEART DISEASE OR AT HIGH RISK FOR ITS DEVELOPMENT: A HANDBOOK FOR PHYSICIANS**, (Dallas, 1975).

Baechle (Ed.) **NSCA's ESSENTIALS OF STRENGTH TRAINING AND CONDITIONING** (Human Kinetics, Champaign, IL 1994)

Brooks, **GOING SOLO: THE ART OF PERSONAL TRAINING** (Moves International, 3rd printing, 1990).

Cotten & Cotten (Eds.) **LEGAL ASPECTS OF WAIVERS IN SPORT, RECREATION AND FITNESS ACTIVITIES** (PRC Publishing, Inc., Canton, OH, 1997).

Cotton (Ed.) **STARTING AND GROWING A PERSONAL TRAINING BUSINESS** (ACE, San Diego, CA 1996).

Cotton (Ed.), **PERSONAL TRAINER MANUAL** (ACE, San Diego, CA 1996).

Ebel, Sol, Bailey and Schecter (Eds), **PRESIDENTIAL SPORTS AWARD FITNESS MANUAL**, (FitCom Corp., Havertown, PA 1983).

Froelicher, **EXERCISE TESTING & TRAINING**, (Year Book Medical Publishers, Inc., Chicago 1983).

Golding, Myers and Sinning (Eds), **THE Y'S WAY TO PHYSICAL FITNESS (revised): A GUIDEBOOK FOR INSTRUCTORS**, (Program Resources Office for the National Board of YMCA of the U.S.A., Rosemont, IL 1982).

Herbert and Herbert, **LEGAL ASPECTS OF PREVENTIVE, REHABILITATIVE & RECREATIONAL EXERCISE PROGRAMS: THIRD EDITION** (PRC Publishing, Inc., Canton, OH 1993).

Jordan (Ed.), **FITNESS THEORY AND PRACTICE** (AFAA, Sherman Oakes, CA, 1995).

THE AMERICANS WITH DISABILITIES ACT: A GUIDE FOR HEALTH CLUBS AND FITNESS CENTERS (Professional Reports Corporation, Canton, OH, 1993).

Parr and Kerr, **LIABILITY AND INSURANCE IN ADULT FITNESS AND CARDIAC REHABILITATION**, (Baltimore, University Park Press, 1975).

Peterson and Tharrett (Eds.), **ACSM'S HEALTH/FITNESS FACILITY STANDARDS AND GUIDELINES, SECOND EDITION** (Human Kinetics, Champaign, IL 1997).

Roberts (Ed.) **THE BUSINESS OF PERSONAL TRAINING** (Human Kinetics, Champaign, IL 1996).

Sol and Gladwin (Eds.), **THE FITNESS PRACTITIONER, AN EMERGING PROFESSION** (AFAA, Sherman Oaks, CA 1997).

THE STANDARDS BOOK FOR EXERCISE PROGRAMS (Professional Reports Corporation, Canton, OH, 1992. Supplemented 1993).

Book Chapters

Legal Considerations, **RESOURCE MANUAL FOR GUIDELINES FOR EXERCISE TESTING AND PRESCRIPTION** (Lea & Febiger, Philadelphia 1988).

Legal Considerations, **AMERICAN COLLEGE OF SPORTS MEDICINE RESOURCE MANUAL FOR GUIDELINES FOR EXERCISE TESTING AND PRESCRIPTION** (Lea & Febiger, Philadelphia, PA, Third Edition 1997).

Legal Concerns for AFAA Fitness Practitioners, **AFAA PRIMER TEXTBOOK FOR THE FITNESS PRACTITIONER** (AFAA, Sherman Oaks, CA, to be published in 1997).

Legal, Professional and Ethical Responsibilities, **ACE LIFESTYLE AND WEIGHT MANAGEMENT CONSULTANT MANUAL**, Richard T. Cotton, Editor in Chief (American Council on Exercise, San Diego, CA 1996).

Legal and Professional Responsibilities of Personal Training, **THE BUSINESS OF PERSONAL TRAINING**, Scott O. Roberts, Ed. (Human Kinetics, Champaign, IL 1995).

Legal Considerations For Graded Exercise Testing and Exercise Prescription, **THE FITNESS BOOK, 2ND ED.**, James A. Peterson, Ph.D., FACSM, Cedric X. Bryant, Ph.D., FACSM (Wellness Bookshelf, St. Louis, MO 1995).

Legal and Professional Responsibilities of Personal Training, **THE BUSINESS OF PERSONAL TRAINING**, Scott O. Roberts, Ed. (Human Kinetics Publishers, Champaign, IL 1994).

Legal Considerations In Graded Exercise Testing And Exercise Prescription, **THE STAIRMASTER FITNESS HANDBOOK**, 83-91 (1992).

Periodicals

American Medical Association, Committee on Exercise and Physical Fitness, "Evaluation for exercise participation: the apparently healthy individual," *JAMA* 219:900-901, 1972.

American Medical Association, Council on Scientific Affairs, "Indications and contraindications for exercise testing (a council report)" *JAMA* 246:1015-1018, 1981.

American Medical Association, "Standards and guidelines for cardiopulmonary resuscitation (CPR) and emergency cardiac care (ECC)," *JAMA* 244:453-509, 1980.

Angsten, "Dance Fitness Standards: To Screen or Not to Screen Participants?," *The Exercise Standards and Malpractice Reporter* 1(1):8-10, 1987.

Angsten, "Overview of Dance Exercise Injury Studies, From Bad to Better: An Industry Improves," *The Exercise Standards and Malpractice Reporter* 2(1):10, 1989.

Angsten, "An Overview of the Standards of Practice for Dance Exercise and Aerobics," *The Exercise Standards and Malpractice Reporter:Lawyer's Edition* 1(2):17-22, 1987.

Angsten, "An Overview of the Standards of Practice for Dance Exercise and Aerobics, Part II: The Use of Expert Witnesses and Standards of Practice in Court," *The Exercise Standards and Malpractice Reporter: Lawyer's Edition* 1(3):36-38, 1987.

Angsten, "Prescription of Activity for Aerobic Dance," *The Exercise Standards and Malpractice Reporter* 2(4):49-51, March, 1989.

Clement, "A Selected Checklist of Risk Management Concerns in Recreational/Sport/Exercise Programs," *The Sports, Parks and Recreation Law Reporter* 1(2):32-34, 1987.

Franklin, "Exertion - Induced Cardio-Vascular Complications: Is Vigorous Exercise Worth The Risk?," *The Exercise Standards and Malpractice Reporter* 2(3):33-41, 1988.

Gerson, "No Pain, No Gain - What's Wrong With Some Exercise Leadership," *The Exercise Standards and Malpractice Reporter* 1(4):52-55, 1987.

Golding, "An Examination of the Standards of Practice of the Young Mens Christian Association (YMCA)," *The Exercise Standards and Malpractice Reporter: Lawyer's Edition* 1(3):29-37, 1987.

Golding, "Standards of Competency For Dance Exercise Instructors," *The Exercise Standards and Malpractice Reporter* 1(3):37-41, 1987.

Hawkins, "The Role of Written Wellness Assessments in Exercise Programming," *The Exercise Standards and Malpractice Reporter* 3(1):8-11, 1989.

Herbert, "A Profile of the American College of Sports Medicine," *The Exercise Standards and Malpractice Reporter: Lawyer's Edition* 1(2):13-17, 1987.

Herbert, "A Review of ACSM's New Standards & Guidelines for Health & Fitness Facilities," *The Sports Medicine Standards and Malpractice Reporter* 33 (July 1997).

Herbert, "A Runner's Death: Suit Against Race 'Sponsor' Results in Defense Verdict," *The Exercise Standards and Malpractice Reporter* 3(1): 27-28, 1989.

Herbert, "An Examination of IRSA's Final Health Club Guidelines," *The Sports Medicine Standards and Malpractice Reporter* 6(6):24 (April 1994).

Herbert, "An Examination of the New ACSM Standards and Guidelines for Health/Fitness Facilities," *The Exercise Standards and Malpractice Reporter* 6(2) (April 1992).

Herbert, "Action For Theft of Member's Property Not Barred by Health Club Release," *The Exercise Standards and Malpractice Reporter* 10(3):38-39 (May 1996).

Herbert, "Another Health Club Release Fails to Protect Facility From Suit," *The Sports, Parks and Recreation Law Reporter* 10(2):24-26 (September 1996).

Herbert, "Appropriate Use of Wellness Appraisals," *Fitness Management* 23, September 1989.

Herbert, "Are Nutritionists Engaged in the Unauthorized Practice of Medicine," *The Exercise Standards and Malpractice Reporter* 2(5):76-78, 1988.

Herbert, "Can GXTs Be Deemed Inherently Dangerous?" *Fitness Management* 29 (June 1991).

Herbert, "Can Published Standards of Care be Used to Judge Conduct Occurring Prior to Standards Publication," *The Exercise Standards and Malpractice Reporter* 9(3):38-39 (May 1995).

Herbert, "Clubs Must Keep Health Related Information Confidential," *The Exercise Standards and Malpractice Reporter* 7(1):8-9 (January 1993).

Herbert, "Clubs and the Rule on Bloodborne Pathogens," *Fitness Management* 38 (January, 1993).

Herbert, "'Dangerous' Bike Costs a Half Million Dollars," *Fitness Management* 37 (February 1992).

Herbert, "Developing A Comprehensive Emergency Response Plan," *The Exercise Standards and Malpractice Reporter* 74 (September 1995).

Herbert, "Dieting Advice Can Lead to Litigation," *Fitness Management* 42, January 1990.

Herbert, "Do Clubs Owe A Duty to Render First Aid or CPR?" *Fitness Management* 23-24 (July 1991).

Herbert, "Do fitness facilities have a duty of referral?" *Fitness Management* 20 (July 1993).

Herbert, "Emergency Response Planning for Strength and Conditioning Programs: Professional and Legal Considerations," *Strength and Conditioning* 16(2):7-9 (April 1994).

Herbert, "Emergency response for foreseeable injuries is legally required," *Strength and Conditioning* 16(1):32-33 (February 1994).

Herbert, "Emergency response may be a requirement," *Fitness Management* 52 (November 1993).

Herbert, "Emergency Response Promotion," *American Journal of Health Promotion* 8(4):272 (March/April 1994).

Herbert, "Equipment Endangers Unsupervised Children," *Fitness Management* 23 (December 1990).

Herbert, "Equipment Injury Trends," *The Exercise Standards and Malpractice Reporter* 2(4): 57-58, 1988.

Herbert, "Equipment-Related Injury Claim 'Barred'," *Fitness Management* 38 (September 1992).

Herbert, "Executed Release Document Bars Suit," *Fitness Management* 44 (January 1997).

Herbert, "Exercise Bicycle Collapses During Use, Plaintiff's Verdict Based Upon Failure to Warn," *The Sports Medicine Standards and Malpractice Reporter* 10 (January 1997).

Herbert, "Exercise Equipment Injury Trends," *The Exercise Standards and Malpractice Reporter* 3(1):25-27, 1989.

Herbert, "Exercise Prescription Without Testing Results in a Plaintiff's Award," *The Exercise Standards and Malpractice Reporter* 6(1):5-6 (January 1992).

Herbert, "Facility Responsibility for Criminal Attacks," *Fitness Management* 20 (September 1995).

Herbert, "Facility supervision: Legal responsibility," *Fitness Management* 22 (February 1994).

Herbert, "First State Licenses Exercise Physiologists," *Fitness Management* 26-27 (October 1995).

Herbert, "GXT Use Raises More Litigation," *Fitness Management* 21-22 (August 1994).

Herbert, "Health Club Release Does Not Bar Suit," *The Exercise Standards and Malpractice Reporter* 10(1):5-6 (January 1996).

Herbert, "Health Club Release Upheld in the State of Washington," *Fitness Management* 36 (May 1997).

Herbert, "Insure Your Success," *ACE Certified News*, 3(3):1 (April/ May 1997).

Herbert, "Is Licensure 'The Future' for CEPs?" *The Exercise Standards and Malpractice Reporter* 10(1):1-4 (January 1996).

Herbert, "Is Litigation In Exercise Increasing?" *The Exercise Standards and Malpractice Reporter* 73 (October/November 1996).

Herbert, "Is Physician Supervision of Exercise Stress Testing Required?," *The Exercise Standards and Malpractice Reporter* 2(1):6-7, 1988.

Herbert, "Is There a Duty to Warn Those Within a Zone of Danger During Recreational Exercise Activities?," *The Exercise Standards and Malpractice Reporter* 1(3):39-40, 1987.

Herbert, "Is There a Legally Mandated Duty to Screen Exercise Participants Prior to Exercise?," *The Exercise Standards and Malpractice Reporter* 1(2):22-23, 1987.

Herbert, "Jogger's Attack In High Crime Area Leads To Suit," *The Exercise Standards and Malpractice Reporter* 5(2):29-30 (March 1991).

Herbert, "Keep Members' health Information Confidential," *Fitness Management* 48 (February 1993).

Herbert, "Keeping Up With the Changing Standard of Care," *The Exercise Standards and Malpractice Reporter* 3(3):37-43, 1989.

Herbert, "Know Your Legal Responsibilities in Administering Stress Testing," *Fitness Management* 16, 67, July/August, 1988.

Herbert, "Lack of Supervision = $ Multimillion Award," *Fitness Management* 19 (August 1995).

Herbert, "Legal Applications in Health Screening Use," *Fitness Management* 19, December 1989.

Herbert, "Legal Aspects of Fitness Management," *Fitness Management* 28, 49, Nov/Dec 1987.

Herbert, "Legal Aspects of Fitness Premises Liability," *Fitness Management* 17-19, September, 1988.

Herbert, "Legal Aspects of Nutritional Advice," *Fitness Management* 19-39, February 1989.

Herbert, "Legal Aspects of Water Based Activities," *Fitness Management* 37, March 1988.

Herbert, "Legal Implications of ACSM's New Facility Standards & Guidelines," *Fitness Management* 20 (August 1997).

Herbert, "Legality of Screening Facility Patrons," *Fitness Management* 16 (December 1994).

Herbert, "Liability for Mere Negligence," *Strength and Conditioning*, Volume 16, No. 6, 27 (December 1994)

Herbert, "Liability Insurance For Health and Fitness Facilities: Making Sure You're Covered – While Knowing What's at Stake," *The Exercise Standards and Malpractice Reporter* 10(3):33-38 (May 1996).

Herbert, "Managing Risk, A more demanding public and closer ties between fitness and health make risk management more essential to health/fitness facilities," *Fitness Management* 45-47, September 1997.

Herbert, "Managing the Risk of Dance Exercise Programs," *Fitness Management* 45, 51, April 1988.

Herbert, "More Exercise Testing Litigation," *The Exercise Standards and Malpractice Reporter* 9(2):23-26 (Spring 1995).

Herbert, "Must Health Clubs Provide CPR For Patrons?" *The Exercise Standards and Malpractice Reporter* 6(1):1-5 (January 1992).

Herbert, "New Health Club Standards From IRSA," *Fitness Management* 23 (December 1992).

Herbert, "New litigation focus on exercise equipment," *Fitness Management* 21 (January 1994).

Herbert, "New Standards for Graded Exercise Testing," *Fitness Management* 42 (April 1991).

Herbert, "New Standards on the Horizon," *Fitness Management* 25 (November 1990).

Herbert, "New Standards from IHRSA for IHRSA Member Health Clubs," *The Sports Medicine Standards and Malpractice Reporter* 37 (July 1997).

Herbert, "Outside Activities Pose Special Concerns," *Fitness Management* 26 (August 1991).

Herbert, "Overcrowding and Poor Supervision Litigated," *Fitness Management* 24 (March 1993).

Herbert, "Owner Not Liable In Use After Closing Time," *Fitness Management* 23 (January 1992).

Herbert, "Personal Fitness Trainers' Higher Duty of Care," *Fitness Management* 23, July 1990.

Herbert, "Personal Fitness Training Standards," *Fitness Management* 27 (March 1992).

Herbert, "Personal Liability in Membership Activities," *Fitness Management* 21 (September 1991).

Herbert, "Properly Drafted Releases Can Limit Liability," *Fitness Management* 24-25 (August 1992).

Herbert, "Prospective Release Bars $ Million Jury Verdict," *Fitness Management* 24 (December 1991).

Herbert, "Prospective Releases Can Really Benefit Programs," *The Exercise Standards and Malpractice Reporter* 11(1):4,5 (January 1997).

Herbert, "Prospectively Executed Release Does Not Bar Suit Against Health Club," *The Exercise Standards and Malpractice Reporter* 10(2):27, 20 (March 1996).

Herbert, "Prospective Releases Must Conform to Law," *Fitness Management* 24, July 1989.

Herbert, "Protection From Claim And Suit in Fitness Activities for Kids," *Fitness Management* 5(3):15-16, March 1989.

Herbert, "Provide Services or Just Facilities? The Legal Concerns are Different," *Fitness Management* 45, January 1988.

Herbert, "Release Bars Weightlifter's Lawsuit," *The Exercise Standards and Malpractice Reporter* 9(1):12 (January 1995).

Herbert, "Sample Informed Consent Forms From The AHA, AACVPR, And The ACSM," *The Exercise Standards and Malpractice Reporter* 5(1):7-9 (January 1991).

Herbert, "Screening Exam Not Unauthorized Practice," *Fitness Management* 50 (November 1994).

Herbert, "Sexual Harassment in Fitness Facilities," *Fitness Management* 24 (March 1995).

Herbert, "Should Health and Fitness Facilities Be Certified?" *The Exercise Standards and Malpractice Reporter* 9(2):17-20 (Spring 1995).

Herbert, "Should Standards Focus on Safety Issues?" *Fitness Management* 17-18 (November 1992).

Herbert, "Standards For Clubs Now 'The Law'," *Fitness Management* 19 (July 1992).

Herbert, "Standards of Practice: Third-party Liability," *Fitness Management* 61-62 (October 1996).

Herbert, "Standards Should be Adopted With Care," *Fitness Management* 22-23 (June 1995).

Herbert, "Stress Test Results In Death and Million Dollar Verdict," *The Sports Medicine Standards and Malpractice Reporter* 4(3):33-36 (July 1992).

Herbert, "Supervision for Strength and Conditioning Activities," *Strength and Conditioning* 16(2):32-33 (April 1994).

Herbert, "Supervision of Children," *The Exercise Standards and Malpractice Reporter* 6(1):7 (January 1992).

Herbert, "Supervising Children in the Health Club," *Fitness Management* 26 (November 1991).

Herbert, "The Americans With Disabilities Act," *Fitness Management* 32 (March 1991).

Herbert, "The Americans With Disabilities Act: Its Application to Health and Fitness Facilities," *The Exercise Standards and Malpractice Reporter* 5(3):70-71 (October 1991).

Herbert, "The Application of Informed Consent Principles to Exercise Stress Testing Procedures," *The Exercise Standards and Malpractice Reporter: Lawyer's Edition* 1(3):43-44, 1987.

Herbert, "The Legal Concerns Associated with the Provision of Unsupervised Facilities," *American Journal of Health Promotion* 183-184 (January/February 1994).

Herbert, "The Liability of Off-Premise Activity," *Fitness Management* 18 (November 1995).

Herbert, "The Provision of More Than Just Facilities for Activity Can Create Additional Legal Concerns for Health Promotion Programs," *American Journal of Health Promotion* 179-180 (January/February 1991).

Herbert, "The Use of Prospective Releases Containing Exculpatory Language in Exercise and Fitness Programs," *The Exercise Standards and Malpractice Reporter* 1(5):75-78, 1987.

Herbert, "The Use of Warning and Instructional Signs in Activity Areas," *The Sports Parks and Recreational Law Reporter* 4(3):41-42 (December 1990); *The Sports Medicine Standards and Malpractice Reporter* 3(1):5-6 (January 1991).

Herbert, "Unauthorized Practice of Dietetics Claims," *Fitness Management* 52 (December 1995).

Herbert, "Update on the Americans With Disabilities Act," *Fitness Management* 30 (October, 1991).

Herbert, "Use of Health Assessments/Questionnaires," *The Exercise Standards and Malpractice Reporter* 6(1):1-6 (January 1992).

Herbert, "Use of Hotel, In-Room Exercise Devices," *Fitness Management* 50 (July 1995).

Herbert, "Use of Weight-Loss Release Upheld," *Fitness Management* 22 (May 1991).

Herbert, "Weightlifter's Lawsuit Will Go To The Jury," *The Sports Medicine Standards and Malpractice Reporter* 8(4):57-58 (October 1996).

Herbert, "What Do Health Club Patrons Expect and Need of Fitness Facilities?" *The Exercise Standards and Malpractice Reporter* 8(6):81 (December 1994).

Herbert & Herbert, "A Window of Legal Vulnerability?," *Optimal Health* 1(4):22-25, March/April, 1985.

Herbert & Herbert, "Equipment Deficiencies and Improper Instruction," *Fitness Management* 12-19, Jan. 1989.

Herbert & Herbert, "Frequent Claims and Suits in Equipment Related Injuries," *Fitness Management* 22, 1988.

Herbert & Herbert, "Legal Implications of Wellness and Health Promotion Programs," *Fitness Management* 210-215, 1988.

Herbert & Herbert, "Reducing Your Potential Liabilities Through Risk Management Services," *Fitness Management* 31-32, 83, 1988.

Herbert & Herbert, "The Legal Aspects of Exercise Leadership in Fitness Programs," *Aerobics & Fitness* 4(1):52-54, 1986.

Herbert & Herbert, "Waivers and Releases," *American Fitness* 38-39, September 1987.

Herbert & Herbert, "Exercise Testing in Adults: Legal and Procedural Considerations for the Physical Educator and Exercise Specialist," *JOPHER* 17-19, June 1975.

Herbert, Herbert & Berger, "A Trial Lawyer's Guide to the Legal Implications of Recreational, Preventive and Rehabilitative Exercise Program Standards of Care," *American Journal of Trial Advocacy* 11(3):433-452, 1988.

Hyman & Feiger, "Legal Aspects of Health & Fitness Clubs: A Healthy and Dangerous Industry," *Colorado Lawyer* 15:1787-1794 (1986).

Koeberle, "Personal Fitness Liability: A Trainer's Guide to Legal Fitness," *The Exercise Standards and Malpractice Reporter* 3(5): 74-79, 1989.

Koeberle, ONE-TO-ONE: "Liability in the Home," *Idea Today* 40-43, April 1990.

Kupcho, "What Is Risk Management?" *The Exercise Standards and Malpractice Reporter* 1(2):26-27, 1987.

Marks, "Is Your Fitness Instructor's Certification Legally Defensible," *The Exercise Standards and Malpractice Reporter* 2(4): 53-56, 1988.

McInnis, et al., "Cardiovascular Screening and Emergency Procedures and Health Clubs and Fitness Centers," *The American Journal of Cardiology* 80:381-383, August 1, 1997.

Rabinoff, "An Examination of Four Recent Cases Against Fitness Instructors," *The Exercise Standards and Malpractice Reporter* 2(3):43-47, 1988.

Richie, "Medical-Legal Implications of Dance Exercise Prescription and Leadership: The Risk of Injury," *The Exercise Standards and Malpractice Reporter* 2(2):17-23, 1988.

Richie, "Medical-Legal Implications of Dance Exercise Leadership: The Aerobic Dance Floor Surface," *The Exercise Standards and Malpractice Reporter* 2(6):87-88, 1988.

Richie, "Medical-Legal Implications of Dance Exercise Leadership: The Role of Footwear," *The Exercise Standards and Malpractice Reporter* 3(4):60-62, 1989.

Sol, "Licensing of Fitness Professionals," *The Exercise Standards and Malpractice Reporter* 4(5):65, 67-68 (1990).

INDEX